GOD'S MISSILES
OVER CUBA

By TOM WHITE

LIVING SACRIFICE BOOK COMPANY
BARTLESVILLE OK 74005

Bible quotations are taken from the King James Version.

God's Missiles Over Cuba
© 1981 by The Voice of the Martyrs, Inc.

Formerly titled Missiles Over Cuba

4th printing, 1996

Published by Living Sacrifice Book Company, P O Box 2273, Bartlesville OK 74005-2273.

Library of Congress Cataloging-in-Publication Data
White, Tom, 1947-
    God's Missiles Over Cuba.
    ISBN 0-88005-000-4

    1. Christian literature-Publication and Distribution-Cuba. 2.
    Persecution-Cuba-History-20th Century. 3. White, Tom, 1947-.
    4. Christian biography-United States. 5. Cuba-Church history. I.
    Title.
Bv2369.5.C9W54
272'.9'097291   81-51935
                                                       AACR2

TO

The unknown brother in Christ who left the mopstring cross in Cell 44, and the millions of God's suffering soldiers whose stories will never be told on Earth. We will meet someday at the feet of our Commander-in-Chief.

Foreword

Two facts stand out supremely in this gripping account of one man's effort to convey the gospel of Jesus Christ to the unhappy nation of Cuba.

The first is the fierce resistance being put up against any form of Christianity in this Communist-dominated land. Despite the misguided attempts of certain North American church leaders to cover up the nature of the persecution, Cuba is here exposed for what she is: a suffering people, dominated by leaders who are as committed to the obliteration of the Christian Church as Nazi Germany ever was to liquidating the Jewish people.

The second fact is the consistency and power of Tom White's witness under fire. Instead of spending his life taking courses or picking black-berries, this young man decided to do something for Cuba. He got into trouble. The reader cannot help admiring his courageous faith under fire. It is truly inspiring.

The author is his own best defender, and I assure you that you will find it hard to put this book down. Meanwhile, let us pray for our neighbors in Cuba, and especially for those who are serving time in wretched prisons simply for taking a stand for God and truth. May the day of their deliverance soon appear. Even so come, Lord Jesus.

Sherwood Eliot Wirt
Editor or Emeritus, *Decision Magazine*

Prologue

T he big Russian truck rolled slowly into the Cuban sugar mill, squeaking and groaning under its heavy cargo. The mill foreman stopped talking with his assistant as he observed the strange load packed tightly on the truck bed.

"There must be some mistake," he mumbled. "What would I do with hundreds of small boxes?"

Noticing the Volga following the truck, he stepped curiously over to the car and tapped on the window. The driver stopped briefly and rolled it down. The little card in the palm of his hand said everything. G-2. Internal Security Police. Called by some the Cuban KGB, it is modeled after the Russian unit. No explanation was needed, and none was given.

As the truck parked beside the huge steel grinders—large drums with hundreds of teeth on them—several workers approached to see what was in the boxes. Noting the stern look on their boss's face, and the plain-clothes men climbing out of the Volga, they quickly turned away. A switch was thrown, and the drums spun to life with a deafening roar. Four soldiers began unloading the truck. As they emptied the boxes into the teeth, the whirling blades ripped and ground and chewed the contents into sweet pulp—but not sugar cane. This sweetness was of a richer nature, for the machine was shredding the words of God, of truth, of light, of love, of compassion.

The mill looms starkly above the flat horizon, surrounded by seas of waving sugar cane. As the Bible pulp burned, a puff of smoke rose lazily from the stack.

One hundred thousand Bibles were thrown into this hungry mouth that day. Only the leather covers were saved, and made into purses.

Dr. Herbert Caudill, a Baptist pastor living in Cuba at the time, reports many such incidents when Bibles and other Christian literature were destroyed. Nothing has changed. Today, more than a decade later, Cuban pastor Noble Alexander and many other Christians tell of the "accidental" burning of 27,000 Bibles in a Havana warehouse after three thousand had been officially distributed, along with the smiles and appropriate photos, for western Christians. In ancient times Christians burned evil scrolls (Acts

19: 18, 19). In Havana, the "evil" burn Christian Bibles.

The threat of missiles from Cuba is one of America's great fears. Cuba's terror comes from missiles of another kind. The Bible is the most powerful force in the world for bringing down the strongholds of evil.

During my four years as a teacher in a Christian high school on Grand Cayman, a British colony south of Cuba, I had been reading books written by Richard Wurmbrand, Haralan Popov, and Brother Andrew. Their accounts of the sufferings and triumphs of Christians under communism gripped my heart. Yet in various church publications, I read stories about the freedom of worship and the abundant literature in Communist lands. Whom was I to believe?

Today one can find pastors or priests either supporting or contesting any given issue. A challenging task was before me. Was I to search for the light of truth or remain comfortably ignorant?

In the summer of 1972 I flew to America to learn more about these stories. From my reading and discussions across the United States, I discovered some of the subtle and overt ways that Christians are persecuted under the Red flag. At a convention in Dallas, I met Reverend Peter Deyneka Jr., whose family was actively engaged in spiritual warfare over the radio. As I traveled and learned more, I sensed that I was "in gear." I didn't know how the gears would mesh, but God did.

Then Michael Wurmbrand described his technique of dropping gospels, sealed in plastic packages, off the coasts of China, Albania, and the Soviet Union. The ocean currents carried them to less accessible areas.

Cuba was definitely inaccessible, an island "imprisoned by chains of water."

This method of distribution is controversial. Some Christian brothers, whom I love, call it wasteful. Perhaps. When possible, tourists or secret couriers could be more effective. Casting God's Bread of Life upon the waters is indeed unorthodox. At a casual glance, it may appear to be stupid. Yet William Tyndale used a similar method to introduce the Word of God to the common man in 16th Century England. He hid the Scriptures in bales of cotton, which were then shipped into the country. Tyndale was burned at the stake for his evangelical zeal. Were it not for his unorthodox methods, English descendants might not have received light until a century later. His Bibles paved the way for the eventual King James translation.

It is easy for Christians on both sides of this issue to accept the Tyndale story because it is history. Hundreds of similar "acceptable" accounts exist. But the approaches of today are more difficult to accept, for we are disturbed by them. Listening to the reports of tyranny and the heroic exploits of believers battling and triumphing over their enemies, we too often do not like to dig, to study, or to pray before taking a position. We prefer to be told what to believe.

During my time in California, I met a Romanian Lutheran pastor, Reverend Richard Wurmbrand, who had suffered unspeakable tortures under the Nazis and the Communists for fourteen years. His wife, Sabina, languished for three years in Communist labor camps.

I am grateful to God that He brought us together. Their constant example of sacrificial love and their selfless dedication to the Body of Christ became a permanent inspiration to me. The Wurmbrand organization's tremendous financial support and prayer support were main forces behind the Cuban gospel invasions. My fellowship with them and with other suffering saints who knew them, provided much spiritual support in dark times.

During the next seven years as I studied the plight of Christians in oppressed countries, believers from Romania, Bulgaria, and Russia would stay in my home. All of them former prisoners for their faith and witness—Vasile Rascol, Reverend David Klassen, and others—would be living stories, not history. These examples of saints under fire would give me courage when I needed it most.

Flying back to Grand Cayman that summer, the airliner roared over Cuba through the established corridor. I remembered my first commerical crossing a year earlier. My Bible, as it had been then, was open on my lap to Psalm 139:9, 10.

> If I take the wings of the morning, and dwell in the uttermost parts of the sea;
>
> Even there shall thy hand lead me, and thy right hand shall hold me.

"What a beautiful, appropriate verse," I breathed.

As with all Scripture, it was to become even richer and more appropriate in future days.

As the jet seemed to lighten in its descent for Grand Cayman, a sense of destiny filled my heart. Below an island of bondage teamed with hungry masses. Desperate for hope and searching for light, they were groping helplessly in their darkness behind the Sugar Cane Curtain.

Who would penetrate that shroud? Who would lift their burdened hearts?

I was ready to volunteer. Did the Scriptures not say, "Cast thy bread upon the waters: for thou shalt find it after many days" (Ecclesiastes 11:1)? The sea would become a carrier of hope, a bearer of light. With the Bible passage "wings of the morning" burning in my heart, yet another realization dawned. Even the sky would yield its message of truth. . . .

Dropping Christian literature from aircraft is not a new technique. Trans World Missions has done this over Mexico and other countries for years. Bill Bright and Dick Halverson tried it over parts of Southern California. Missionary pilots in jungle areas have dropped presents, pictures and leaflets. This highly unorthodox method of evangelism draws fire from some sectors of the Christian community. Perhaps some of the fire is justified. But much of it is not.

Some have wondered if my imprisonment

may have been just In the free world, what would we do to Communists who littered our countryside from the sky with literature, they ask. But there is no need for that approach in the lands of liberty. The Communists print their material openly in many western countries. Christian literature is not printed in their homeland.

My seven years of periodic literature drops over and around Cuba was no flash-in-the-pan James Bond type activity coated with a thin verbal gloss of "in the name of Jesus." It was a concerted effort to penetrate the island of fear with the gospel of love.

Some view the smuggling of God's Word too exotic for Christian endeavor. "Why be a James Bond and defy the authorities?" they argue. "Let's keep this kind of thing under control; there are legal ways. After all, the Apostle Paul says we should respect the authorities. God ordains the rulers, does He not?"

It is not the purpose of this book to discuss this issue. Nevertheless I must take a stand.

All Christians must obey and respect the authorities. In every area that is Caesar's, we must give to Caesar. But some things do not belong to him.

In Jesus's day, the authorities feared that the living Christ would place them in a politically unstable position. They twisted spiritual issues to make them appear political. This deception was the deciding factor in Jesus' death. "If we let him . . . alone," they reasoned, " . . . the

Romans shall come and take away both our place and nation" (John 11:48).

On another occasion Peter and the other apostles stood before these same men and challenged, "We ought to obey God rather than men" (Acts 5:29).

In committing treason against her country, Rahab obeyed God's higher law by letting the spies down over the wall (Joshua 2:15). In Hebrews 11, God honored her faith.

The Book of Acts declares that Paul went to Jerusalem, and later to Rome, in bonds. He willingly submitted himself to the authorities, but only because he knew it was God's plan (Acts 19:21; 21:13, 14; 23:11). We need spiritual wisdom to know when submission will further the ministry and when it will hinder. Paul, who preached submission in civil matters, often fled from authorities who sought to destroy God's work.

Paul defines what an authority is in 1 Timothy 2:2, Romans 13:3, 4, Hebrews 13:17, and 1 Peter 2:14. Throughout history, God has *conditionally* supported authorities according to those definitions. He has no respect for them, however, when they disobey Him. The Pharoah was punished with plagues. Herod died in agony because of his apostasy. How many times did God cross civil law and liberate His followers from jail in the Book of Acts?

The continual fulfillment of the Great Commission is our primary task. This is our highest calling. But God began to use Samuel, then

David with Jonathan, to bypass Saul's spiritual authority. Because King Saul "turned back from following me, and hath not performed my commandments," God rejected his sovereignty (1 Samuel 16:1-3, 15:11). On this Scriptural basis, Communist authorities are not recognized in God's eyes. Smuggling Christian literature is not illegal, for God is our supreme authority; He has commissioned us to go into *all* the world with the gospel.

Unfortunately, we in the west are inconsistent in our thinking concerning the Christian-governmental conflict. Why do we approve Christian short-wave radio broadcasts into Communist lands, but abhor various "smuggling" techniques because it looks dark and deceptive? What is the difference between the spoken and the printed word? When our radio broadcasts penetrate the Soviet Union and Cuba, are they legal in Communist eyes? If so, why have the Soviets spent billions of rubles on high-powered jamming systems in these countries?

Moralistic terminology can trick us into intellectualizing the situation. I have learned of hungry sheep who are not getting food, and Jesus said, "Feed my sheep." I have learned about a country, Cuba, which officially accepts a religious pill but spits it out by destroying Bibles. If the sad, sick patient won't take a pill by normal means then, like concerned doctors, we must use a "horrifying, unorthodox" method, which strikes terror to the heart of many a child. We must give an injection directly into the bloodstream.

Ironically, many Christians, as well as Communists, attack the smuggling of literature on the same point. "You shouldn't mix politics with the gospel," they contend. "You should just preach the pure gospel."

John the Baptist lost his head because he applied the gospel to Herod's sin of marrying his brother's wife. Stephen, the first Christian martyr, was stoned because his "pure gospel" accused the Sanhedrin of murder. The light of truth enlightened some while exposing others. It is not a positive or a negative light, a religious or political light. As God's pure searchlight, it penetrates every area of our lives. The world does not enjoy the glare of exposure, for light painfully reveals the darkness of its evil. Nevertheless as children of the light, our mission is to penetrate the world with the brilliancy of God's truth.

To that end, I dedicate this book. Mine is not the story of the triumph of a person over a system. It is a testimony of God's conquering love, of God's faithful protection, of God's patient instruction in an ideological hell.

I am indebted to the family of Richard Wurmbrand and The Voice of the Martyrs for the concepts, literature and financing which made these Cuban operations possible. The prayers and support of Christians across America keep the torch burning in the darkest corners of the world.

Contents

Tom and Ofelia White
Dorothy and Daniel

1

"Eight Zero Juliet... Mayday! Mayday!

N ight was falling as we approached the Cuban coast at our first radio beacon checkpoint over Punta Alegre. Mel Bailey was battling to hold the trembling plane on course in spite of a strong, turbulent crosswind. As we began the forty-five mile crossing, I forced the rear door of the Cherokee Six open and propped it with pieces of cardboard. Because of the pressure of the air against the door, I quickly abandoned my intricate plan of dropping a certain quantity of gospel literature every minute and simply began working as fast as I could. We would have only twenty minutes over land. Bracing myself and breathing a prayer to Jesus for strength, I began cutting the strings of the five pound bundles and tossing them out.

Meanwhile, Mel was having trouble communicating with Havana, and had switched frequencies to talk with Camaguey.

"Camaguey Center, this is Cherokee Eight Zero Juliet. What is your weather over Cuba?" he called.

" . . . Zero Juli . . . No signifi . . . weath . . . visibility . . ." the radio crackled with static.

"Camaguey, we're approaching a thunderstorm. Can you give us vectors around it?"

"Negative . . . Eight . . . 'ro Juliet," the controller responded weakly.

"Do you have us on radar, Camaguey?"

"Negative . . . Zero Juliet," the voice returned.

Perhaps the storm nearby blocked us from their screen. Below us I could see the lights of houses, automobiles and streets, like tiny jewels twinkling in the darkness. Would the tracts be found? Would they be read? Would the good seed of God's love and hope be planted in the hearts below? I had no way of knowing but, despite its turbulence, the wind was a great blessing in God's plan. We were about to learn the answers to my questions.

We reached the southwest coast of Cuba, crossing exactly at the outbound radio beacon checkpoint of Simone Reyes. Just as we left land I had dropped the last bundle of literature.

"The tracts are all gone!" I shouted to Mel triumphantly.

"Hallelujah!" he yelled, waving his right arm joyously.

"Ooo-eee! Thank you, Jesus!" I laughed.

The plane bounced more severely now as we drew closer to the storm over water on our southern leg to Jamaica. I began to clean the strings, cardboard, and tape off of the floor. Sitting in the rear, I was nauseated by the swaying. *Well Lord*, I thought, *if all it takes is a little throwing up, then You can include that anytime.* Mel was threading his bucking bronco through the lightning, winds and thunderheads. Finally climbing into the co-pilot's seat, I began to realize just how serious our problem was. We were now communicating with Kingston Center.

"Eight Zero Juliet, do you have DME?"

"Negative, Kingston," Mel returned. "Do you have radar?"

"Negative, Eight Zero Juliet."

"What's the weather at Montego Bay, Kingston?" Mel shouted.

Up ahead I could see the line of storms between us and Jamaica. Center transferred us to Montego Bay Approach Control, but it couldn't help us either. Mel banked the plane left to go around the storm. The number two VOR (a navigational aid) went dead, and number one was unreliable. Our ADF (Automatic Direction Finder) needle was spinning wildly. Ahead loomed what looked like an island, and Mel depressed his mike switch.

"Montego Approach, Eight Zero Juliet. Jamaica possibly in sight. VORs malfunctioning."

"Roger, Eight Zero Juliet, we're flashing runway lights. Do you have us in sight, sir?"

"Negative." Mel and I strained forward close to the plexiglass, scanning the black, rainy night meticulously. No runway.

"Turn on your landing lights, Eight Zero Juliet," the calm voice instructed.

Mel flipped a switch. On and off. On and off. On again. "Do you see us, Montego?" His voice reflected growing tension.

"Negative, Eight Zero Juliet."

The roaring motor continued to suck precious drops of gasoline. The four fuel gauges were directly in front of me. Two of the red needles were pegged on empty. The other two were dangerously close.

Suddenly we saw a patch of light off our left wingtip. Was *that* Jamaica? If so, we were passing it, heading out to open sea. We had life rafts and survival equipment, but ditching in such stormy seas at night would surely get us killed! With such pressure and uncertainty, we banked left and headed like a moth drawn to light.

Suddenly the engine sputtered and fell silent. Another needle moved onto the empty mark. Instinctively, Mel switched to the fourth tank, and the motor burst into life again. I flicked a worried glance at Mel as he picked up his mike again.

"Montego, we're heading toward a light. Fuel nearly gone."

"Roger, Eight Zero Juliet. We're still flashing runway lights. We'll send a fire truck to the end of the runway. Look for its emergency beacon. Do you copy?"

"Affirmative, Montego."

"Eight Zero Juliet, when you reach the island, follow the coastline. You should be able to find the airport. You may descend to three thousand feet."

With the coastline passing below, we strained to locate the beacon. All we could see were little villages. Their strings of tiny lights along the shore appeared like a necklace.

"Eight Zero Juliet," the controller's voice faded slightly in the static, "do you see the fire truck?"

"Negative, Montego," Mel answered grimly, fighting the buffeting controls. "And we have about five minutes of fuel left. . . ."

"Eight Zero Juliet, please flash your landing light again."

Our light, a tiny spark in the murky sky, flashed on and off, on and off, to unseeing eyes as we flew up and down the coast. Suddenly the static-plagued radio crackled loudly and fell silent as a flash of light zig-zagged across our path.

"Let's land on that highway . . . fast." I jabbed a finger at the fuel gauges. The engine had already stopped three times on three empty tanks.

We were low enough to see people along the coastal highway gazing up at our obviously distressed aircraft.

"Land on that road? Look at the people

This Cherokee Six was used on one of the gospel flights. It is identical to the plane which crashed in Cuba.

standing on it!" Mel gasped incredulously.

"They'll get outa the way," I yelled frantically. "We land or we crash!"

I prayed fervently as Mel made a final low pass, trying to clear the road. Hoping that he could still transmit on the radio, he switched to the emergency frequency.

"Mayday. Mayday. Mayday! Cherokee Five Five Eight Zero Juliet. Mayday!"

Hand once more on the throttle, Mel eased back on the power and lined up with the highway for a flawless landing approach. He slipped under the lights and planned to touch down ahead of a dump truck which had been parked on the side. As Mel pulled the nose of the Cherokee up into touchdown position, he lost sight of the vehicle. I raised my hands to warn him, but it was too late. With arms in front of my face, I whispered the most powerful name on Earth—*Jesus*—just as we struck the truck at about seventy miles per hour.

The wheels were still about a foot above the highway upon impact. The right wing was sheered off a few feet from my shoulder. The plane spun around, twisting and tumbling for a quarter mile down the road before the other wing ripped away. Much of the plexiglass was broken out as we bounced upside down, tumbled, and skidded to a stop right side up.

"Get out! Get Out!" Mel yelled, fearing a fire.

Tearing at my seatbelt release, I pushed open the door and we dove into the warm tropical night. Voices speaking excitedly in Spanish quickly surrounded us. Horrified, I turned to Mel.

"This isn't Jamaica. It's Cuba!"

It was 1:20 in the morning of May 27, 1979. My wife's birthday. For a fleeting moment, I longed to be home, in Glendale, California, to be near her, to touch her. . . .

Our aeronautical spectacular had taken place in front of G-2 police headquarters. A Russian-

made motorcycle with a side car roared up
through the crowd. Mel and I were immediately
placed on it and whisked off through the streets
of Manzanillo, a coastal town in the province
formerly called Oriente. Mel and I had little time
to speak together. Roaring down the center of
the road with the wind in our faces, I was simply
grateful for being alive on solid ground with no
more airsickness. *Hang on to Jesus, and take
each moment as it comes with Him,* I thought.

We pulled up to a dilapidated building and
were taken inside. It was a hospital. We still were
being treated as tourists, for the Cubans had not
yet realized our nationality. We sat in a tiny
examination room, Mel opposite me. Removing
our life vests, and feeling around our bodies, we
both became conscious of God's mighty protection and grace. We had not one scratch or bruise.

"The King of the Universe was riding with us,
Mel," I smiled happily. "He'll continue to be
with us, even in Cuba."

The halls were lined with people as we left the
building. *That's strange,* I mused. *Why are so
many people waiting to see the doctor at two in
the morning?* We didn't realize until later that
they were waiting to get a glimpse of us.

Outside, we were led to a Russian car and
driven through town. One of the passengers in
the front seat was reading a piece of literature. A
few hundred gospel tracts had stuck to the tail
of the plane and, during the crash, had been
scattered all over the highway. *Could he be
reading one of them?* I shuddered. We stopped

at a little house to wait for immigration officials and the G-2. In the living room, I scrawled my wife's name and address on a scrap of paper and tried to give it to a woman in the kitchen, knowing it might be the only chance I would ever have to contact my family.

"Please, ma'am, please send this to my wife," I pleaded.

She raised her hands in front of her as if under attack, her eyes wide with fear.

"Nothing bad is going to happen to you," she shrieked.

"Please," I persisted.

"No, No! Nothing bad is going to happen."

"In the name of God, please take it!" I demanded.

She lowered her eyes and shook her head. I walked apprehensively back into the living room.

We were hurried to immigration and inter-rogated at length by eight or nine officials.

"Where were you going?" they demanded. Mel and I sat together on a sofa, facing them.

"We were going to Montego Bay, but got lost in the storm," Mel answered calmly.

"So, you were *just* going to Jamaica for the weekend like tourists, huh?" a moustached man behind the desk scoffed. He picked up one of the plastic-coated gospels and smiled, blowing a long stream of cigarette smoke in front of him. "So, some of this just *happened* to fall out of the plane on the way across, *si*?"

I glanced toward a man standing by the wall across the room. He was wearing a green military uniform, and he was talking fervently on the phone to Havana, describing the literature in his hand. My heart sank with the realization that we would be in Cuba for quite some time. Guards ushered me downstairs to the lobby as Mel was questioned further. Feeling exhausted, I rested my head on a desk and tried to sleep.

I had just closed my eyes when a lion roared. In Cuba . . . a lion? Again the roar. I raised my head and asked the guard, "Is there a zoo nearby?" He nodded. I put my head down again and smiled. Daniel. He had a few conflicts with a government, but God was with him. I thought of my son Daniel, too. The biblical Daniel had impeccable manners and respect for civil authority, yet when that authority crossed the line into God's territory, Daniel obeyed God rather than men. In that moment, the prophet's witness gave me strength.

Mel and I were kept separate when the Cubans realized that we were more than just tourists. Policemen drove us in different cars to a small airport where our smashed aircraft had been taken on a truck. As a boom on the truck placed the "remains" of the plane on a concrete slab, we once again marveled at God's grace. While the officials examined the plane and its contents, I sat on the concrete, propped against a steel girder, trying to get more sleep. But the mosquitoes wouldn't let me. I slapped at them in the damp, cool air, but there were too many and their attacks were relentless.

Taking pity on me, an old guard let me sit in

the side car of his police motorcycle. He was short with a tan, leathery face and protruding ears which curled out from under his military hat. A simple man with a wide, foolish grin, he frequently rubbed his rough, stubby fingers across his face to wipe the sleep out of his bloodshot eyes.

"Did you know that there is a God and that He loves you?" I asked quietly.

He flapped his hand as if to bat away those words and mumbled, "Science has proved that we come from the slime, the amoeba."

"But haven't you ever looked into the faces of your children and marveled at the miracle of their likeness to you, of the millions of cells which came to form a nose and eyes that look like yours?"

"Ha! Children are only a sexual product." He grunted, glanced furtively toward the other guards, and put his finger to his lips in a gesture of silence. *He doesn't want to appear friendly with me in front of the others*, I thought. I still pray for him.

Mel, meanwhile, was explaining the different uses of the survival equipment, which was now spread out on the concrete slab around the battered fuselage of the wingless Cherokee. Many curious policemen, G-2, and rural guards gathered around him as a few officials went through the papers we had on board.

"This is an emergency locating transmitter," Mel intoned. They clustered around the suspicious looking boxes and packages with various expressions of respect, fear and delight. One guard carried his Russian assault rifle like a toy. Some of the guards reminded me of stories I had heard about the early visits of the Auca Indians with Nate Saint on the sand bar in Ecuador.

I joined Mel in the laughter at times, as he told jokes to his spectators. "You see," Mel grinned, "we only have one survival radio which is tied to *my* equipment. If we ditched in the ocean, Tom had better be swimming with me." I happily translated for him, relaxing a little. *How could these people be dangerous*, I wondered hopefully. *We might get away from here as tourists yet!*

As the sun rose slowly, I watched trucks full of old men and young women rumbling toward the sugar cane fields. It was Sunday morning. *Are those the "volunteers" I've heard about, who are rounded up from churches and put to work?*

Mel and I were allowed to rest for a few hours before we were returned to the crash site. Our escorts pointed out where we hit and how far we had skidded and rolled. About a dozen elementary school children walked curiously past us. I put my fingers in the curly hair of one little boy, wondering if he would ever hear of Jesus as Savior.

Returning to the hotel to eat, I experienced my first encounter with Communist incongruity. As we sat at the table, someone brought the menu to us. On the left, the list of food was on old yellow spotted paper. A few poor dishes were offered, consisting mostly of rice. On the right side was a spotless new sheet of typing paper, listing chicken, pork chops, and whole fish. It obviously had been placed there for our benefit.

Clearly delighted at being able to order the pork chops, one of the guards in our entourage ate it as if Christmas and Thanksgiving were rolled into one. Later we learned that little meat was available for the common people. Protests and demonstrations would surface across the island during the time that we were there, due, in part, to this.

After lunch we were packed into a small Alfa Romeo with some police. A guard sat between Mel and me; we were forbidden to visit. The car went screeching around curves as it left the poor town of Manzanillo. The last memory I have of the town was that of a store window with one dress hanging in it and some plastic apples. Although I had lost my glasses in the crash, I was still able to see the poverty.

The driver was pushing the little car to the limit as we covered some eighty miles to Holguin. I had heard the word *airplane* mentioned and, sure enough, we roared up to an airport. We darted through the open gates to the steps of a Yak-40 Russian-made Cubana Airlines passenger jet. Mel and I boarded the plane, each under a G-2 guard. After fastening my seatbelt, I looked back at Mel sitting in the rear and half-jokingly said, "Looks like we have our own private jet."

But soon other passengers boarded, looking at us curiously. We had held up their flight for more than two hours. It seemed strange to me that not one person complained. In this totalitarian system, when police are present, none dare gripe. I could imagine what passengers on a U.S. airline would say to someone who had delayed their flight for so long. Freedom of speech guarantees the right to gripe.

As we flew toward Havana, a man and his wife (or girlfriend) sat in front of me. They were openly affectionate. At one point he whispered in her ear, touching her on the back of the neck, and laughed at a private joke. It was then that I felt the hurt, almost a physical pain, of knowing that my precious wife was home alone, unaware of what was happening to me. My head slumped against the window. I prayed for Ofelia and the children. The bay area of Havana came into view. Without my glasses, I couldn't make out the finer details of the city. Nevertheless, my thoughts turned to our gospel tracts. *What a beautiful place to drop literature.*

We deplaned last, the cold reality of the situation hitting us as we were handcuffed and taken to G-2 headquarters. Driving through the big gate with the high walls, chainlink fences, and barbed wire, we entered what had formerly been the Villa Marista, a Catholic monastery. It has been converted into the interrogation headquarters of Internal Security—the G-2 political police, many of whom are "secret" or plain clothes agents.

In the conversion of this building, I perceived a physical manifestation of the spiritual warfare of Satan against the church. I remembered reading Karl Marx's devilish black magic poetry, which he wrote as a university student. The cells in this building were formerly used for prayer. Now they were used to squeeze and torment men's minds and souls.

We were stripped, given a detailed body search, and sent up to the second floor for our sleeveless yellow overalls, the former uniform of Batista's forces. I was thrown into Cell 44, Mel into Cell 60.

My main concern was sleep. I lay back on the thin, lumpy mattress that covered a board held to the wall by chains. I rolled from side to side, but no sleep came, for my body was not yet accustomed to the hardness. By now, I was rapidly realizing that God wanted me in Cuba. Our unusual crash was no accident from His standpoint. But why? What good could come from rotting away in a Communist prison? What had become of the tracts we had dropped?

My mind drifted to happier times, to a small island in the Caribbean far from my dark, lonely cell. . . .

2

BREAD OVER
TROUBLED WATERS

G rand Cayman is a picturesque little island of waving palm trees and white beaches surrounded by crystal clear water. The memory of its small family-knit population of quiet, smiling faces brought warmth as I lay on that back-breaking bed in Cell 44.

I thought of my little apartment there, which had become a warehouse for plastic bags, soda straws and chewing gum, and of the beginning of my smuggling adventures.

Several Christians, including a fellow teacher named Art Manchester and a few dedicated students, met with me on Saturdays to package gospel tracts, assembly-line fashion. We packed the literature, together with a straw and a stick of gum, in the bags and heat-sealed them. The

chewing gum would attract children or others on
the beach and induce them to open the package
and then remove the literature. The straw would
keep it afloat.

In one country Christians patrol the beach for
such literature. Was Cuba different? Would our
planned gospel seadrop be in vain? Would we
ever know? By the winter of 1972, we were
ready to learn the answers.

We stuffed the 50,000 packets into big plastic
trash bags and hauled them aboard a boat in
Georgetown Harbor. The evening was clear, and
the moonlight danced happily on the water as
we weighed anchor. The low, white office buildings seemed to be moving away as we slid over a
calm sea until the island resembled a dollar-size
pancake on the horizon. Soon we were alone.

Watching this scene from the roof of the pilot
house, I finished my huge salami and cheese
sandwich and lay back to gaze at the stars. It
was my first trip at sea. *Not bad, not bad at all*, I
thought, listening to the steady throb of the
engines. *This is beautiful.* Below, three Christian
brothers were still eating and laughing with the
crew.

Captain Alfred Eaton had set a course parallel
to Cuba, carefully staying in international waters
twelve miles off the coast. We wouldn't reach
our drop zone until the next day. Everything
seemed perfect. I was nearly asleep in the warm
Caribbean night when the boat began to lunge in
rough water. Spray flew over me, twenty-five
feet above the sea. Scurrying below, I learned

that we were going into a northwester, a seasonal storm. Within thirty minutes all we landlubbers were seasick. In a few hours the crew joined us. The captain and Art were the only two who rode this wild horse without ill effects.

All night the boat headed into the storm. Rearing up on crests of turbulent waves, then smacking into the troughs, we lurched along in a jerky but constant rhythm. All the beds were taken by sick men. I lay on a wooden bench which was nailed to the wall near the galley table. Every ten minutes or so I would heave.

After four or five hours, Art swayed into the kitchen.

"The Captain wants to know if you want to turn back," he announced, holding on to the table. "He says we'll probably have this weather for the rest of the trip. He wants to know what you want to do."

I slowly pushed myself up into a sitting position, then staggered and weaved to face him. Great doubts came upon me. *This is crazy! Am I a Jonah on a stubborn, fruitless mission? It probably won't work anyway. But we are halfway to our destination, and I am halfway there in my faith.* Definitely not feeling like a hero, I shook my head and managed to say between heaves, simply "No!" On we plunged.

By morning light the storm had eased, and we were nearing the drop area. We decided to leave a line of gospels about fifty miles long, dumping more heavily at the last point. I sat up front and began throwing packets into the sea—praying

This fishing boat carried God's love on the waves of the sea.

that the Lord, whom I felt had inspired this effort, would bless this little offering and use it.

Art and Bob Johnson came forward and began dumping in heavier quantities. It was easy to rip open the boxes and big plastic bags as we lifted them up to the rail. Thousands of packages poured out, fluttering over the swells, and leaving a white trail behind us. The wind that had given us a bad night was now moving the literature in a broad pattern. The deck was slippery. We staggered and fell often because of the swells, but we managed to complete the drop.

We could not see Cuba. It was a cloudy day and we were twelve miles off shore but, by radar and LORAN navigation, we knew our position. Poor Frederick Pritchard, the third brother helping us, never made it out of bed during the trip. I was definitely in a position to sympathize with him! After finishing the drop, we turned around and lay on the captain's bed for another thirty-six hours, arising every few hours only for water.

On the return trip an oil tanker in Cuban waters spotted us and turned toward us as if it would ram our boat. Passing too closely for comfort within Cuban waters, he evidently was afraid that we were Cuban. We were fearful that he had hostile intentions, since he was not flying a flag and refused to communicate on the radio. His massive bow, cutting through the sea, came nearer—a hundred yards off. Our captain loaded his 30-30 rifle as a last resort, though it would be useless against this mountain of steel. But it

proved to be a question of curiosity for both
parties. The tanker passed just behind us. We
were thrilled to see Georgetown again.

A few months later, thirty-six Cuban refugees
in a small fishing boat sought refuge on Grand
Cayman. Although Cuban military planes had
searched for them, dropping flares at night, they
had arrived safely. I drove out to the beach
house which the Cayman government had provided. Tubal Cain, a high school Spanish teacher
and my interpreter, strode with me across the
white sand and into the little wooden house.
The refugees were sitting in tired, nervous
groups on the bunk beds and at a card table.

"God bless you," I greeted through Tubal.
"Would you mind if I asked some questions?"

They nodded and invited us to sit.

"I am interested in the life of the Christians in
Cuba. Can you tell me something about it?"

A tall, thin, dark-haired girl, Lucia Reyes,
walked up to the table where we were seated.
"At my church we would try to have a youth
service, but the authorities would always bother
us," she offered.

"What do you mean? Would they throw rocks
at the building?" I probed.

"No, but every time we would start the service, a big truck would roll up outside the door.
The military would stand on the steps asking for
volunteers to cut the cane. We soon learned that
the only time they wanted us to volunteer was
when we met to worship. Everyone must go, or
you are unpatriotic." She sank slowly onto a

bunk bed, hands clenched tightly.

A short, plump man with moustache and glasses came forward on his own. Angry words began to pour from his mouth as if they had been dammed for many years. "I have tasted the freedom of religion in Cuba! The freedom of the Castro Communist government is to close every church in my town!" Dr. Enrique Alvarez was breathing heavily, finally able to let it all tumble out. "The only religion is Fidel Castro. Fidel . . . Fidel . . . that's all you hear anymore!"

"It is impossible now to obtain a Bible," another refugee blurted. Brushing a hand across his eyes, he drooped against the wall and continued, "Everything is falling apart, the books, the churches . . . it's all falling apart."

"Look," I responded hopefully, "we made a boat trip a few months ago. We went here. . . ." I drew a rough map on some paper. "Did you ever see any literature in plastic packages?"

I looked around the dingy, dark room at the forlorn figures, hoping for at least one smile or nod of recognition. But no. They had seen nothing. It would be seven years before I heard anything.

During Easter vacation in the Spring of 1973, I flew to San Jose, Costa Rica, with some of the students from our Spanish class at the Triple C School where I taught. I didn't speak a word of the language at that time, but I went to help chaperone the group. One night, during a Christian service in a large home in the mountains, I met Ofelia. After the service, I gave my address to some of her sisters who wished to write me. She was standing silently against the kitchen wall and smiling. Something leaped inside me.

The next morning, confident that there were enough teachers to chaperone the students, I took the first bus from San Jose back up to the mountains. My new-found friend and I couldn't understand each other, but there are so many kinds of languages! Sitting on the big veranda in the warm sun, we took our Bibles and began "speaking" to each other. The first few days we were in the Psalms and Proverbs. We would take our Bible on the buses everywhere. The compassion, tenderness and purity of the Spirit of Jesus in her would witness to the Jesus in me.

Near the end of that beautiful week, as God's Spirit was confirming some things in our hearts, we read portions of the beautiful love poetry in the Song of Solomon. At times it was funny! Her father, a strong Christian, would walk up to us on the porch, and I would be embarrassed and stop reading. She would laugh heartily and tease, "Don't stop, keep reading!"

I would visit the shop where she worked as a seamstress and sit by her machine, ignoring her girlfriend's giggles. After only a week to see each other, I reluctantly returned to Grand Cayman.

For seven months we wrote, more than a hundred letters a piece. When I learned that her girlfriend had to translate my love notes, I immediately began sweating it out in Spanish. I could imagine that the little valley where her family had lived for three hundred years was delighted in learning of the romantic expressions sent every day by the amorous American.

Missionaries there highly recommended Ofelia and me to each other. On that encouragement and on the foundation of our Lord, we planned to be married in December of 1973. She had visited Grand Cayman once with her sister for a few weeks, and I had visited her home.

I remember the morning I crossed the river below her house to where her father was working at Hogar del Buen Samaritano, a Christian retirement home. Her mother was the director. I intended to ask him for permission to marry his daughter. Nervously, I practiced my lines as I strolled along. In my practically non-existent Spanish, I would be trying to explain to him that his daughter was to be spirited out of Costa Rica to a tiny island, far away from her family. Now, looking back, I feel sure he knew why I was crossing the bridge. Perhaps the whole valley knew!

We engaged in some small talk for a few minutes beside a tree. With our limited vocabulary, it was definitely "small" talk. Francisco, or Pancho as he is called, is a dedicated servant of the Lord. I took comfort in that. If he let me down, it wouldn't be with a crash. After I awkwardly communicated my wishes, he smiled quietly and spoke, "Although Ofelia will be away from us and away from her mother, I know that she will be in the hands of the Lord."

He said more, but at that time this was all I

could understand. I shook his tough hand,
thanking God for his tender heart.

Years earlier he had helped some Mennonite
Christians build this retirement home. Previously
he had been one of the wealthiest men in the
valley but, through drinking and loose spending,
he had lost it all. One of the Christians gave him
a Bible. He decided to read it cover to cover to
check it out before choosing to believe in a
personal Savior. After coming to the Lord, he
brought many in his family to the feet of Jesus,
and he still ministers as a lay pastor. Today
Pancho illustrates the thought, "A rich man is
seldom satisfied, but a satisfied man is always
rich."

In the summer of '73 I decided on one more
boat trip and began preparing 100,000 packages.
It wasn't time to be looking for fruit; God
seemed to be saying, "Keep sowing seeds." All
through the long, hot days of June and July, I
prepared packages, again with some faithful
students: Roy, Stan, Kim, the Reynolds and
others. Knowing that the ocean currents have
seasonal changes, I planned to return to the
same location for a varied pattern. As we neared
the target date, I learned that the boat was not
available. What was to be done? While continuing to seal packages, I prayed for a way.

Somehow the Lord sent me to a Christian
pilot, Carlton Bodden, who agreed to fly me
across Cuba through the established air corridor
to the Bahamas. I would simply drop half the

Carlton Bodden, right, flew the first air drop over Cuba. The door broke in flight, possibly causing the inspection by suspicious Cuban air force pilots.

load before crossing the southeast coast and the other half after crossing the northeast coast.

Early Sunday morning, August 12, Carlton and I took off from Grand Cayman in a twin engine Beechcraft D-18. The ten seats had been removed to accommodate the cargo. We were loaded with forty large plastic bags containing about 70,000 leaflets sealed in plastic. They filled the passenger section of the fuselage. We left the remaining 30,000 or so behind, planning to use them later.

As Carlton taxied to the end of the runway, I squirmed and crawled across the bags to the emergency window. The voice of the Cayman tower operator crackled on the radio, "Cleared for takeoff to Congo Town Airport in the

Bahamas. Climb and maintain 7,000."

Carlton shoved the throttles forward slowly, and the roar of the big twin Pratt & Whitney engines filled the cabin. I reached up and jerked the release lever on the window, pulled the window panel inside, and laid it the bags. The wind tore at my shirt as I watched the cows and palm trees flash by. We lifted off and began climbing. Cuban airspace laws require a pre-clearance before flight, so they knew we were coming.

"Boyeros, this is Beech Niner Seven Niner Zero Zulu," Carlton called Havana Control. No answer. He glanced at the radio and checked the frequency. Yes, 126.9.

"Boyeros, this is Niner Seven Niner Zero Zulu, over. . . ."

Still no reply. He banked the plane in a wide circle as we waited contact for permission to cross. For ten minutes he tried in vain to raise Havana. What happened? Did they know we were circling? Were they coming for us now? I scanned the horizon and the sea. All I could see was a bright blue sky, and a green and turquoise Caribbean dotted with some little cays off the south coast. Finally the faint voice of the Havana controller crackled over the radio. ". . . Niner Zero Zulu, proceed to Simones beacon as requested." We leveled off, and headed toward the island twenty-five miles away.

I began pouring our gospel literature through the emergency window opening. The large thin plastic trash bags tore easily in the 140 mph wind after I ripped them a little. Half of the load went down in this area until we neared the coast. Joining Carlton in the cockpit, I tightened my seat belt and relaxed. Smoke from the sugar mills and the green countryside of Camaguey province was plainly visible below. Carlton talked from time to time with Cuban air traffic controllers to keep them informed of our position.

Suddenly we heard a great whooshing noise. Peering back into the cabin, I saw that our large back door had fallen open and was hanging below the fuselage. One of its two restraining cables had broken. There we were, flying in the brilliant Sunday morning, a door blown open, an emergency window out, and about a thousand of the leaflets being sucked out over the towns and cow pastures. The large plastic sacks had inflated when we climbed to altitude, and the strings had popped off. Thousands of the leaflets were free, blowing like snow around the cabin. Had I not been in the cockpit at the time, I would have been skydiving without a parachute.

When Carlton saw the amazed expression on my face, he half turned in his seat to look aft, shaking his head in disbelief.

"I'll go back, Carlton. Maybe I can do something," I offered.

"No, wait! Let's clear the other coast first."

Calmly, Carlton keyed his mike and continued talking to Havana.

"Havana, Niner Zero Zulu continuing to

Andros as requested. Proceeding to Alegre Beacon."

Perhaps Russian-made tracking equipment was observing us from below. Although the plastic probably wouldn't show up on radar, we considered the possibility of mounted telescopic cameras—the kind used to follow missile launches. We had launched "missiles" of our own. Would they detect them?

As we approached the northeast coast near Moron, and were preparing to dump the remaining twenty sacks, a gray object flashed by our left side and did a tight roll ahead of us.

"Wow! Look at that!" I pointed for Carlton, who couldn't help but see the Russian-built MIG. A second fighter stayed one hundred yards behind on the right, watching, locked on to our flight path.

Although we knew the situation was dangerous, we had peace in our hearts. I was surprised at my calmness. It was not one of ignorance, but one which seemed to say, "Relax, son, everything is under control."

On the surface things couldn't have been worse! I started to leave the cockpit for the cabin to destroy certain papers in my briefcase. "No, wait, Tom," Carlton advised. "We might get away okay. Let's see what they do."

"Here he comes again!" I shouted above the roar of our engines.

The screaming jet on our left pulled in so close that I could see the pilot's white helmet. He repeated his maneuver several times, each pass going as slowly as possible.

"Carlton, he's trying to look inside!" I yelled. "Do you think he can see anything?"

Carlton continued on course as though he had not heard me. We certainly looked suspicious with the door hanging down, but the MIG pilot also could see the broken cable.

Miraculously the packages had settled to the floor, seemingly on their own, as if a band of angels were sitting on them! Had the material continued to blow out the door when he passed by, all would have been lost.

The fluttering cable evidently assured the pilot that we had an accident. Not once did we receive radio communication from him or with the ground during that ordeal. He must have been reporting to them on a military frequency.

Dropping off into a left bank, he suddenly left. We flew on another five minutes. I climbed into the cabin and, taking off my glasses, thrust my head out the emergency window. The other MIG had left, too. They had gone! Thank God, we were free. I quickly unloaded the remaining materials.

As Carlton reduced our flying speed, I leaned out the doorway to pull in the door. When I grasped the cable, the flex in the rubber-coated cable and the heavy hanging door nearly propelled me into a headlong dive into the Caribbean. I let go and jumped back. Realizing it would be impossible to land with the door hanging below the fuselage, I braced a foot against each wall beside the doorway and jammed my forehead against the low ceiling for another attempt. I was able to pull the door in, but at the expense of losing a little hair!

As I lay on my hard, wooden bed in Cell 44, my mind tried to picture Carlton. He was a quiet, strong man who never complained or spoke harshly. He disappeared the next year as a co-pilot on a private flight to Florida with three other men.

I often pondered what happened, and now my thoughts pictured those tense seconds just hours ago before Mel and I crashed on the highway.

Mel? What was happening with him? I'd almost forgotten him in Cell 60. Why were we being kept apart? Would I see him again?

My body ached from stiffness, and I tried to shift to a more comfortable position. Sleep seemed as far away as . . . as that tiny island that once had been my home. Slowly, my mind wandered to a more pleasant time when I was captured by a sweet, calm, quiet little Costa Rican angel. . . .

3

In the School of the Spirit

I t was December, and our wedding day was fast approaching. A few days before the ceremony, I flew from Grand Cayman to San Jose and took a taxi to Ofelia's house. The big wooden door swung open late at night and I kissed her mother, then Ofelia, in one of those rare kisses! Almost always during our courtship, we were chaperoned by one of her sisters. But since we were in our mid-twenties at the time, I didn't mind. It was natural and pleasant.

Once Ofelia and I went with her aunt and two little children up on the mountainside of a lush green coffee plantation to pick rose apples and look at the coffee plants. We walked hand in hand through the rows of tall mature plants with rustling leaves. Morning dew was still on the grass, and the air was fragrant from flowers. We stopped at a little clearing beside a tall tree. We still could speak very little. Thoughtfully, Ofelia's aunt took the cousins farther ahead. Ofelia leaned against the tree and smiled. I looked down at her dark brown eyes and long hair flowing gently across her neck.

"You're very pretty" I breathed, my lips feeling a tug toward hers.

She laughed. I bent down to kiss her.

"Tomás, Tomás," she whispered quietly. I held both of her hands and we touched noses. Soon the others rustled back into our area, making sufficient noise to alert us. The kids were great, snapping sticks, yelling, playing— better than alarm bells. Early the next morning I went alone up the mountain and carved our initials into the tree with a machete, a long knife much used in Latin America. I carved the cross of Jesus between our initials.

The night before our wedding we had a delightful celebration at Ofelia's home, with a serenade. All of the relatives and neighbors were invited. Missionaries Harry and Jean Nachtigall kindly interpreted the events for me. The women and girls were inside the house while the men and boys stood outside on the big veranda. Four or five musicians stood in front of the closed door and sang to the women, symbolizing the love of the groom for the bride. The songs rolled throughout the night and, with my broken Spanish, I tried to sing with them. The soft lights, fingers flashing over guitar strings, the smiles, laughter, and joking made a lovely evening. But for me the loveliest thing waited behind the closed door.

The little window in the door squeaked open. I strained to see Ofelia, but the lights in the living room were out. All I could see were six or seven noses as the women happily watched their concert from the darkness. When would I see her? Finally, the moment was at hand. The door swung open, and my smiling Ofelia met me. We kissed. Everyone cheered. It couldn't have been more romantic!

Our wedding was at the *Seminario Latinamericano*, one of the oldest and most respected seminaries in Central America. My Christian brother, Alson Ebanks, played his guitar while I sang to Ofelia. More than 250 guests attended the ceremony and, later, a large banquet of chicken and rice. Ofelia looked a little tired after the wedding. I learned later that she had made her own wedding dress and all of the bridesmaids' dresses in the last weeks before the ceremony. Flying back to the island the next day, we now had a bilingual New Testament. We read it together as the Lord gave us patience and love while we built our vocabulary.

During the Christmas holiday, Ofelia and I flew in a DC-3 with Steve and Ruby Smith to Cayman Brac. The plane stops at times on romantic Little Cayman, population fourteen then, using a grass runway. It has beautiful quiet places, with white and pink beaches.

We climbed cliffs on Cayman Brac, explored

caves, drove slowly down the one main road, and visited with the island's most beautiful attraction—its people. We stayed in the two back rooms of a tiny church at Cotton Tree Bay. That Sunday, Ruby played the piano, Steve and I spoke, and Ofelia (not yet speaking English) smiled and allowed the Holy Spirit to share her love without words.

Settling down to our ministry on Grand Cayman, I decided to continue the literature projects until I received word from Cuba. Similar outreaches had received replies through the mail, although often it was years later. In 1974 I was able to give most of the sacks of literature remaining from the last two trips to the crewmen of a commercial ship. This was done with the knowledge of the shipping agent. He was able to distribute the packets along the international shipping route passing the Cuban coastline. He later told me that a Cuban torpedo boat followed him for some distance near to the points where he had dropped the literature. But the Gospels were not disturbed.

Two areas of love grew equally fast in my life! That of teaching in a Christian school, and that of studying the struggles and victories of the church in Communist countries. What was to be done? How would God direct? I was greatly disturbed by the fact that official Christian publications and international church conferences were not revealing the truth. Not only did they fail to cover the persecution which exists in these countries, but they proclaimed that it did not exist.

Cuban and Russian pastors coming to the Free World on official tours proclaimed complete freedom. Yet in not one case that I know of did they bring their families with them. Why? This probably made it harder for them to defect, should they ever choose to do so and thus be able to tell the whole truth. Exiles Solzhenitsyn and Georgi Vins, the Baptist minister, both freed, held back partially after their coming to the United States until their families were safely out of the Soviet Union.

Some of the visiting pastors are sent to deceive us. During Vins' imprisonment, I confronted Michael Bichkov, who was then president of the Russian Baptists and was visiting a large midwestern city. I asked him before the television cameras why he claimed that Vins was imprisoned for "income tax evasion." Vins' father, a pastor, had died in prison. Was this, I asked, another "tax problem" case? He dodged the question, as well as many similar ones from the audience.

"Why was my own Bible confiscated at the Moscow airport?" an elderly woman asked.

"Bibles must be officially presented," was the stiff reply.

A young girl stood and asked, "Why was Nijole Sadunite imprisoned in Lithuania for printing a religious newspaper?"

No answer. Of the fifteen questions presented in the sanctuary of the big church, Bichkov skillfully sidestepped ten. A man with a Slavic

accent sitting in the audience stood and began
screaming, "Lies . . . lies . . . you are not telling
the whole story!"

Bichkov calmly stood there while the ushers
dragged the man down the aisle to the door.

Remembering this incident, I wondered,
*couldn't I do something constructive to offset
this deception?* But there was so little time. As
my responsibilities with the school and church
in Cayman grew, so did my concern for Cuba.
Things were building to a critical point. Also a
new arrival was coming to our home!

In July of 1975, Dorothy Elizabeth White was
born during a summer visit with my parents in
Dallas, Texas. Ofelia's parents also were there
for the birth. I thought surely my wife would
have a boy, in which case I would be on familiar
territory. But I was literally floored by such a
beautiful little thing when I saw Dorothy in the
nursery. I sat on the floor in the hall with my
brother, Jim, and some friends. We watched her
for hours. I wouldn't trade her for ten boys.

Soon we were boarding a jet with this precious bundle, returning to our little Caribbean
bungalow where I began my fifth year of
teaching. Once again I prepared happily to
teach, direct the plays, the church cantatas, and
continue my work with Cuba. But God had
other plans. The day before school began, I
became extremely weak and pale. At the hospital the doctor discovered massive internal bleeding. Since I hadn't been a good steward of my
body and slowed down, I simply broke down. I

was too weak for an operation. But God graciously spared my life, and the bleeding stopped. The next several weeks were spent in bed, where I reconsidered my priorities. Always caring, my mother flew to see me.

In the fall of 1975 I sadly left Cayman to rest in Ofelia's parents' home. It was a refreshing time of physical activity in the mountains, with the early misty mornings, the milk cows being led down the street, and Ofelia's joyful family always singing little choruses of praise to God as they worked.

Once I ventured to the seminary where we had been married. What a shock! The long bulletin board was covered with red paper. Paper soldiers holding machine guns were tacked to it. Above them was the slogan, "We are united with our Nicaraguan brothers." Walking over to it, I wrote across the paper a reference from Matthew 26:52: "They that take the sword shall perish with the sword." The school was now financed by the World Council of Churches.

Conditions were changing fast. Liberation theology sweeping Latin America was shifting the spiritual-social concept of the gospel far to the social side, thereby deceiving and entrapping many. A professor at the seminary later told me that, because of their humanitarian works, Argentine revolutionary Che Guevara and the Indian leader Mahatma Ghandi were closer to Christ than most Christians! What the professor—and those he is leading—did not recognize is that true social justice and liberty is the result of

spiritual rebirth. Without a proper relationship
with God through Jesus Christ, all human
attempts at social improvement are doomed to
fail. Why? Because it is not a social battle we are
fighting; it is titanic spiritual warfare between
God and the forces of Satan.

Sensing that God was moving me to take a
deeper part in answering His call to arms, I
decided to commit myself fulltime to active
duty.

Selling most of our wedding presents, we flew to
Glendale, California, to work with Christian
Missions to the Communist World. Here I was to
meet fresh and living examples of Christians from
Cuba, Eastern Europe and Russia, those who are
still in the furnace and coming out of the fire. The
tiny percentage who make it to the West represent
only the tip of the iceberg. My reading and studying
was about to be confirmed. I learned much from
the quiet people, the unknown heroes who will
never be seen on television, heard on radio, or write
a book.

One such visit was that of Vasile Rascol and
his family. Ofelia had flown with Dorothy to
Costa Rica to visit her family for three weeks, so
I, not liking to spend my time in the kitchen,
was eating out of cans and boxes in lazy bach-
elor style. A sweet Romanian family came to
California just in time. The mother, Elena, was a
fantastic cook! They spoke little English, but by
now I was used to such language handicaps, and
we communicated nevertheless.

Vasile, the father, had sad, dark eyes but a

The Rascol family on the day of Vasile's release from prison.

smile illuminated his face. He had just been released from two years of prison in Romania, part of a four-year term for distributing Bibles to other Christians. Elena had fought constantly for his release. He showed me the great scar running down his leg where, the day after surgery in the prison hospital for varicose veins, his stitches had ripped open and were not reclosed. The guards only laughed at his cries for help. The problems in his legs developed because his cell was too small in which to walk.

His twelve-year-old son, Dorian, and six-year-old daughter, Christiana, were unusual children.

The Communist state forbids the distribution of
Christian literature. Dorian would stand on the
street corner watching for the police, while
Christiana would run from house to house pushing Christian tracts under the doors. This
reminded me of the early Christians praying in
the Roman catacombs. They rendered unto
Caesar, a self-proclaimed god, in civil matters,
but remembered the Prophet Isaiah's words concerning Jesus: "The government shall be upon
His shoulders."

This quiet, beautiful family had many stories
to tell. They are tales which will never be written in a book, but they hit me with the force of
a living Book of Acts. What the apostles suffered
was normal Christianity. Today, western Christians live under a special umbrella of protection,
a blessing given to us by God for a time, for His
purposes.

The next "apostle" to visit my home was a
Baptist minister, David Klassen, who had just
left ten years of Russian labor camps. While he
was in a camp praying, the picture of Lenin
would be placed in front of him.

"Look!" they would mock him, "you are
praying to Lenin!"

Once, in camp number 243 of Northern Russia, a guard set his attack dog on Klassen. David
was praying as the vicious Doberman raced
toward him. Suddenly the dog turned and
jumped, not at him, but at the guard, biting his
master's rifle. Other guards ran to help the pale,
frightened guard.

Once at a labor camp in Bulgaria, Christians were placed in a pit with other attack dogs. The dogs became nervous and began whining and scratching on the dirt wall, trying to escape . . . like Daniel with the lions. Such stories are almost common among the saints in prison.

Reverend Assen Simeonov, the former representative of Bulgaria to the World Council of Churches, stayed in my home. He told of a World Council meeting in Kenya when the Soviet Bloc representatives were told by the Russian delegates to vote "together" on the issues. He was astonished at the power-plays and behind-the-scenes maneuvering. Simeonov quit the World Council and held a seminary in the woods outside of Sofia for Christian young people who wanted to serve God.

Simeonov told me that, like all others in Communist countries, the Bulgarian seminary had a dry, spiritless body of intellectual professors who only emphasized the mutual points of "agreement" between Marx and Jesus. Another pastor attended such a seminary in Romania. Only by obtaining a key from a sympathetic person was he able to hide in the library at night and read about the great saints and Church fathers from books kept in locked cabinets.

During 1975 through 1978, I was able to visit with many such people. Their simple stories were published at times in a monthly newsletter of the mission or partially in a magazine article or newspaper story. But the details, the delicate human aspects, were living realities before my eyes. These people ate with me and prayed for me. Ours were not brief tourist encounters, designed to create a carefully prepared impression; we lived together as brothers for long periods of time.

One final story. Once, when Vasile and Elena were taking the Bibles to the Christians—Bibles printed by our mission in Europe—there was a day of heavy snow in Bucharest. Although cars were not allowed on the street, they had to meet a Christian missionary to receive twenty-eight sacks of Bibles. Vasile and Elena went with his brother in a big empty city bus. Plowing through the deep white drifts, they finally stopped behind the waiting car, blocking the street. After a few hugs and kisses with the missionary, the rapid transfer began. Twenty sacks of precious cargo made it into the bus.

Suddenly, Vasile saw the flashing light of a police car behind them. He and Elena quickly jumped into the bus and lay on the floor. It belonged to the *securitate*—the special political police, similar to the Russian KGB or the Cuban G-2. The officer parked behind the bus and stepped slowly toward the two vehicles, his long shiny black boots pushing through the snow.

Vasile's brother quickly threw open the hood of the bus and pretended to make repairs. All were praying silently. The policeman said nothing. As he breathed heavily from the walk, clouds of warm air puffed from his open mouth. He jerked the door of the missionary's car open and peered inside, his hand resting on the remaining sacks of Bibles. Seeing nothing suspicious, he turned abruptly and sloughed his way back to the patrol car.

"Thank you, Lord Jesus," Elena whispered as she watched him from the window.

Many are the stories of God's protection in times of peril—even in America. On July 2, 1976, I was driving on a Los Angeles freeway when, without warning, I began to heave blood. Traveling in the fast lane, I tried to work my way over to an exit, but had no time. As everything began to grow dark and dizzy, I whispered "Jesus" and collapsed. The car was destroyed in the ensuing accident, but I only received a small cut on my cheek. The paramedics rushed me to California Hospital, where the doctor heard air passing through my heart. He called to a young intern in the emergency room.

"Hey, come over here and listen to this guy's heart. I want you to learn this." He waited for the medic to listen with his stethoscope. "Do you hear that swish, swish sound? That's when the heart is not receiving enough blood and air is passing through." The medic adjusted and readjusted the cold instrument but didn't seem to hear it.

The surgeons found several things wrong, including cancer—a type that is rarely lethal. But they couldn't find the primary tumor. Lying in the bed after surgery, I felt peaceful in the quiet room. The heavy curtains were slightly open to allow a ray of light across the bed. It was beautiful, golden.

As my head rested on the pillow, I began to hear music. First came the sopranos in crystal clear high notes which echoed as if in a great cathedral. Soon the altos, tenors, and mighty deep bass joined the anthem. Verse after verse of praise filtered down over my bed like the sunlight. Enthralled, I didn't want it to stop. After about fifteen minutes, the singing faded, but the joy remained.

Later, I told Mother, who was there as usual in a crisis, about the singing. She cried, believing that I was about to die.

"Mother, I'm not dying," I tried to comfort her. "I can't go to church, so God was just giving me a special concert."

During the next few years, I received a valuable education, reading religious and political publications from around the world. Daily I was able to compare many different statements and photos and form my opinions and convictions, and not simply from one story or one camp. One of the strongest proofs of widespread religious persecution came from the Russian newspapers themselves.

Over and over again I would read of the arrests of Baptists, Pentecostals, Orthodox, and Adventists, and accusations of the "poison" they spread. I reviewed transcripts of their trials, which were mockeries of justice. Then in official religious publications of the West, I would read statements by leaders that these persecutions did not exist, or that "their crimes are of civil nature because we have been assured by the Communist authorities that this is the case.''

I began to see by these comparisons how valuable is the Bible verse that says, "Study to show thyself approved." I wasn't becoming a doubting Thomas in spiritual areas, but I *was* becoming a cautious, skeptical, and studious Thomas. I was in a "boot camp," studying anti-subterfuge warfare. I had to learn to recognize Satan's deadly deceptions, which he practices daily on ignorant humanity. It occurred to me that Westerners truly want to believe the best of people. While this is an admirable trait, when carried to the extreme it becomes willful ignorance.

Once again I focused on Cuba. We had received no word, so I presumed that all of the sea drops had been ineffective. Since the Spanish congregation at our church was about half Cuban, I was still much in touch and concerned. Our pastor was Dr. Juan Oropesa, a minister who, because of his faith, had spent seven years in Fidel Castro's prison. Aware of a lack of Christian literature in Cuba, I recalled the one trip I had made over land and the accidental distribution of packages out of the Beechcraft's broken door. An intriguing thought flashed into my mind. *Why not again, but at night?*

In faith I ordered the printing of more than 100,000 portions of Christian literature. I discovered that if these pieces were laminated in Mylar plastic, they would be practically indestructible. One piece could be passed around a hundred times with no tearing, fading or deterioration.

At home in our living room I gave a sample piece to my son, Daniel, for the toughest test possible. He was at the chewing age, so one might say that he cut his teeth on the gospel. After one week of jerking, biting and flapping, he produced only a few creases and dents, but the material was perfectly legible and whole, and there were no cuts.

One night Ofelia and I drove down to the beach at Santa Monica carrying an empty five gallon gasoline can. (It is evident that my wife is a patient, longsuffering woman.) We scooped up gallons of seawater to take home for my experiment. I couldn't use fresh water; it had to be the real thing!

Taking some of the laminated literature, I first chopped it into pieces then tossed it into the water in our kitchen sink. Sweet Ofelia said nothing about the sand, salt water smelling like diesel fuel, and paper in her otherwise spotless kitchen. The next morning everything was floating nicely, and the chopped pieces had absorbed no water. The paper was so thin that the laminating plastic under heat and pressure had cooked its way through it. Cutting it from the great press sheets would present no problem.

During this test period, another Christian pilot, a Baptist minister, took five boxes of these Gospel portions and dumped them out over

Pilot John Lessing and Tom White discuss flights to Cuba.

international waters at a place we felt to be useful. Still no word from Cuba.

Finally, not knowing when or with whom, I began planning a night flight across the island of Cuba. My pilot, John Lessing, brought the appropriate charts to my home, and we began to plan the mission—load, airspeed, distance, fuel. Night after night . . . phone calls through lunchtime . . . every fiber of my body was alive with this project. Praying for guidance, I lived it, ate it, slept it. Waking up at two and three in the morning, I would go to the dining room where the big aeronautical chart was spread on the table. I would pray, figure distance, time, fuel stops, even how to open the back door of the plane we did not yet have. It was as if I had been preparing for this during my entire lifetime, led by a sovereign God.

In December, after a year of nights and week-ends working on the details, we were on our way. Because he lacked the necessary instrument rating needed for crossing Cuba, John found another pilot to go with us. Linda Jackson received her rating the day before the flight.

Crew of the Bay of Pigs gospel invasion

4

Manna from 10,000 Feet

We had registered with Havana by telegram, as required, giving our plane number, pilots' names, and date of crossing. On December 7 we made a fourteen-hour flight around Cuba from Fort Lauderdale, Florida, along the Bahama chain, then south of Cuba to Georgetown, Grand Cayman. Our yellow and green single-engine Cherokee Six was a good load carrier.

Landing in Georgetown that evening, I had little time to say hello to friends. We had only a forty-five minute fuel stop before we would head for Cuba. Our plane was not inspected, since we were in transit. I ran up into the tower to see my friend, Jeri Andrews. Working with a lady flight controller and a lady pilot was a new experience for me. Having no knowledge of our intentions, Jeri cleared our flight through Kingston, Jamaica, radio, which in turn checked with Havana. All was in order. We had permission to cross.

As we taxied to the runway, I began opening the boxes back in the cabin. In the tropical humidity, I was immediately drenched in sweat. John and Linda checked the instruments and took off at the required time. Jeri's voice came over the radio as the plane climbed to our assigned altitude, "... cleared as filed to the Hollywood-Fort Lauderdale Airport. Maintain 9,000."

"Roger, Georgetown," Linda acknowledged routinely.

Our first beacon check-point was located ironically at the Bay of Pigs or Giron, Cuba, where the military invasion of the sixties had taken place. The first thirty minutes of the flight went as planned. Linda calmly spoke one last time to Jeri.

"Reporting at ATUVI intersection, level at 9,000."

With clouds and no ground references, it was a black evening, and the pilots were forced to rely solely on instruments. Jeri signed off with, "Contact Boyeros radio on 126.9."

We were still an hour from the Giron radio beacon when Linda noticed that the directional gyro had to be reset to the magnetic compass every few moments. This wasn't normal. She flicked a nervous look at John.

"This is thirty degrees off course, and I just reset it a minute ago," Linda complained.

This was not the time for navigational problems. John jabbed a finger at the ADF. It was tuned to the Giron radio beacon, which would guide us to the coast. Shaking his head, he strained to hear the Morse Code beeping noise. It was too faint. Meanwhile, a strong crosswind was pushing us off course. By the time we arrived over Giron, we were fifteen minutes late. Linda was furious. Seeing lightning in the clouds, John was justifiably nervous. He feared it might be the strobe light of a MIG fighter.

We crossed the Bay of Pigs, heading directly for the opposite radio beacon on the north coast at Veradero. *A second invasion*, I thought, *but of a different nature.* As we neared the point where I would begin dropping literature, it dawned on me that this was Pearl Harbor Day. I prayed that the messages of love we were dropping would have the effect of spiritual bombs to encourage the Christian, while planting a seed of questioning in the mind of the Marxist.

We were carrying a specially written gospel tract for the Marxist. Prepared by a former atheist, now a Christian pastor, the tract simply pointed out that if one follows the footsteps of Marx and Lenin, all ends in the grave, since there is no belief in life after death. It proclaimed that neither Marxism nor Capitalism offers the eternal hope that Jesus Christ gives. Only through acceptance of the sacrifice of Jesus can the soul find love and peace and hope.

To be effective, literature must be understandable. To the Marxist mind, it must be explained. Jesus said in Matthew 13:18, 19:

> Hear ye therefore the parable of the sower. When any one heareth the word of the kingdom, and *understandeth it not*, then cometh the wicked one, and catcheth away that which was sown in his heart. . . .

Our literature used the concept of the gods of Marx and Lenin to introduce the one true God, Jesus. Paul used the Unknown god to introduce Jesus. The Christian literature introduced most often into Communist countries is the Bible. But for the hardened Marxist-Communist, we also have discovered that *In the Footsteps of Marx and Lenin* and other simple booklets like *What Christians Believe* (also sent to Cuba) are effective and not thrown into the trash at first glance. It opens the door, prepares the soil. Before the Sanhedrin, Paul used the life after death issue to present Christ. So we present it to the Marxists. It's the same gospel, the same love, but it's in a personal package.

After four or five minutes on course over land, I popped open the back door and placed a wedge of foam rubber in the crack. Taping an earphone to my right ear, I listened to the recording of a metronome precisely ticking the seconds. I began throwing the literature out in a timed rhythm. On this trip we were not sure if the Cubans had the type of radar which would detect this. Nevertheless, I fed the material out in a thin stream as recommended by a Christian physics professor, Dr. Larry James, who had studied the situation in his university laboratories.

I was pleased to see that, although we were not passing directly over any towns, the countryside was more populated than the chart had indicated. Half the time we were sailing over little house lights, street lamps, and other signs of civilization. Our little love missiles fluttered into the darkness like snow, whirling and spinning as they slowly floated to the earth.

Linda calmly continued talking with Havana Control over the drone of the engine. We passed the northern radio beacon exactly on course, and I dumped the heaviest load near Matanzas on Veradero Beach, the most famous in Cuba. The tall lighthouse there was swinging its sharp beam through the night, cutting into the thousands of leaflets settling over the sand and water.

We signed off from Havana and switched frequencies to Miami Center. As the plane hurried away from Cuba, I thought of the next morning when the literature would be found all over the ground. I remembered the passage in Exodus

16:14, 15 about the manna, which fed Israel in the wilderness.

> And when the dew that lay was gone up, behold, upon the face of the wilderness there lay a small round thing, as small as the hoarfrost on the ground.
> And when the children of Israel saw it, they said one to another, "It is manna," for they wist not what it was. And Moses said unto them, "This is the bread which the Lord has given you to eat."

I prayed that His bread would be eaten.

By now we had distributed more than half of the laminated material. But a great quantity still lay in my garage in Glendale. Though we had saturated the air corridor of Giron, the air corridor called the Maya still lay untouched. I had flown this same corridor over Camaguey province with Carlton in 1973. Because the Giron trip had passed without mishap, we believed that the remaining literature could be dropped in heavier quantity on a pass over the Maya.

John wouldn't be able to go on this trip because his name was registered on the pre-flight clearance telegram filed in Havana from the Giron flight. We wanted to take no chances. Praying and hoping for another instrument pilot to help me, I began taking flying lessons.

For the first few weeks this was hard on Ofelia. She had lived through my times in the hospital, the danger in the flights I had made, and was now obligated to endure my new adventures in a seemingly fragile trainer which looked to her like a toy. In comparison to a commercial air carrier, I guess it was! Dismayed, she stood beside it on the ramp and shook the entire plane by the tail.

"When you crash in this thing, I'm leaving for Costa Rica!" she stormed.

"Oh, come on Ofe, these things are safe. Don't you know how much engineering went into these instruments?"

I opened the door of the trainer to show her, but she wasn't impressed.

Fearing for my safety and wanting security for our children, she threw away my registration papers for flight school one night shortly before classes were to begin. Unable to find them, I dumped all of the garbage onto the kitchen floor looking for them. Amazed, my little Dorothy stood in the doorway and, in her sweet three-year-old voice, asked about the trash.

Stubbornly, I continued thrashing around in the mess, mumbling something soothing to her, then drove hurriedly back to Glendale College to register again for the class. Many nights after that I would roll over in bed and find Ofelia's face wet with tears. None of my reassurances calmed her fears nor satisfied her need for security.

In a few weeks she appeared to accept the

fact that her husband was to be a pilot. But God had other ideas. I definitely am not pilot material. Though my ground school and ten hours of practice proceeded smoothly, somehow I sensed it would end in failure. I could probably pass all the tests eventually but, when facing difficulties or unexpected problems, I knew that my mind would not be able to handle the split-second complex technical decisions that might have to be made. Not wanting to suffer a loss of face, I refused to quit. So circumstances made the decision for me.

Sitting in our living room after an evening class, I felt nauseous and stepped quickly to the kitchen sink. Within seconds I was filling it with pints of bright red blood. Weak from the ordeal, I struggled to the bedroom.

"Ofelia . . . have to . . . go to the hospital. The sink is full of blood," I spoke quietly.

A neighbor came to be with the children. Ofelia started up our Volkswagen and whisked me to the little hospital near our home.

"Tom, maybe if you weren't doing so many things . . . if you would only slow down," Ofelia suggested, changing lanes to pass a slow moving truck and trailer. Her hesitant remark broke a long silence between us. I continued to lean my head against the car window and keep my eyes closed.

"Yeah," I sighed. "The flying lessons. I'll have to . . . quit."

In Community Hospital I was again on an emergency room table. Ofelia sat on a little stool beside me, hands folded, watching intently as the kind man in the white coat shoved tubes down my nose and throat. He spoke with a Slavic accent.

"Where are you from? Eastern Europe?" I choked the words out. "My sister-in-law is from the Ukraine."

"I'm from Russia," he smiled and began to insert a needle for the intraveinous solution into my arm.

"How did you get out?"

"I was at a medical conference in Canada. I had to leave my wife and children behind." His forehead knitted into a sad frown. "She is still there . . . my beautiful wife. She has blond hair."

I felt great pity for him. I was bleeding internally but at least my wife was sitting beside me. He was bleeding in another way. The doctor moved me upstairs for observation for a few days. The bleeding stopped once, but then it began again. Back down to the emergency room. A gastroscopic tube was forced down my throat, but there was too much blood to see anything. Suddenly, great fountains of it began gushing out of my mouth, my body temperature began to drop, and my legs shook violently.

"We need nine units of blood down here, fast!" a doctor ordered sharply. Two others attempted to start a transfusion, slapping on my veins to find one that wasn't in a partial state of collapse.

"Where's that blood?" the doctor yelled.

"Didn't somebody call? I need it now!"

A nurse came to wrap a warm blanket around my legs, gently holding them down with her hands. I heard a voice, "Everything's going to be okay, honey." Another nurse held my hand as I kept retching.

"Oh, God," I silently prayed. "I'm nobody . . . but if You could just keep me alive for Dorothy and Daniel . . . They are so little . . . Don't let them grow up without me. Please, Jesus."

I felt myself being wheeled out of the room, into the hall, into an elevator and up. The word "surgery" passed through my ears, then all went dark. . . .

Later, in the fog of intensive care, I drifted under sedation. I sensed that Mother was there with Ofelia. She whispered in my ear, "I'll take care of the children."

The diagnosis was cancer again, this time of the stomach. Thankfully, it was a small tumor, which the surgeon removed. Feeling much like a beached whale, I once more lay under the sheets with tubes and lines and monitors attached to me. My brother, Jim, flew in from Dallas with my other brother from New York, and we had a few happy reunions in the hospital room. Jorge Garcia and Reverend Larry Swain came and prayed. Then I had a few weeks of rest in the hospital while my stomach healed.

I wanted so badly to see my children! One night Ofelia smuggled them up to my floor. The nurses didn't seem to mind. My stomach tube was tied off temporarily, with one foot of it protruding from my nose. With baby Daniel on my lap and my wife and Dorothy by my side, I spent some blissful moments in the waiting room. Daniel loved the tube. I would flap it in front of him, and he would grab and try to chew on it. Ofelia would fly to the rescue.

I had much time to pray and consider the future during those quiet days alone. My pilot books and Bible were by the bed. I turned to Psalm 139:9, 10: "If I take the wings of the morning, and dwell in the uttermost parts of the sea, even there shall thy right hand lead me. . . ."

"Oh, God, what do I do?" I prayed. "It is physically impossible for me to continue this work."

Then the verse came, "I can do *all* things *through Christ* which strengthened me" (Philippians 4:13).

One evening I observed a man, who appeared to be Latin, mopping the floor. As he swished from side to side down the hall, I spoke to him in Spanish, telling him something about Cuba. He turned out to be Cuban himself. Excited, the custodian called an elderly cleaning woman to meet me. Their eyes shone with tears, so grateful were they that an American from California would be concerned about their island so far away.

We said goodbye, and I shuffled on down the hall in my slippers and robe, whistling, "A Mighty Fortress Is Our God." It was late at night. I couldn't sing because my abdominal muscles were still healing, but at least I could whistle. The burden and love for Cubans, people starving for a word of love—God's love—came upon me. I stopped at a phone cubicle recessed into the wall and cried.

"Oh, dear God, give me one more trip, just one more trip."

The tears rolled down my face. I knew I couldn't quit. He knew it, too. If we open to Him, He becomes our before and our after. The desires He delights to create in our hearts He also enjoys to fulfill.

A few weeks later, I wrote to Mel Bailey, a Christian and former Army captain, and a helicopter test pilot. He also was proficient in fixed wing aircraft. We set a tentative date for the Memorial Day weekend to make the crossover through the Maya corridor.

Mel began looking for a plane on the East Coast, since he is from Virginia, and I began planning the timing of the literature distribution. With my body still weak from surgery, I began a serious program of vitamins, health foods, and light exercises. Meanwhile, I tied the literature into five-pound bundles for easy handling, using Ofelia's dishwashing gloves for a sure grip.

Three times a day I would take a five-pound bundle in each hand and lift it hundreds of times to develop better muscle tone for the flight. I would have to be able to toss with my left arm, in twenty minutes, seventeen box-loads of five-pound packages after cutting the string on each.

Hundreds of pounds, in perfect coordination. Only three months would lapse from operating table to cross-over flight, but I was confident of God's help.

The night before I left California for the reunion with Mel on the East Coast, Ofelia helped me load the van. This would be our longest, most dangerous flight. Though legally registered with Cuba, we still would be flying in a single engine plane over hundreds of miles of water at night.

The morning of my departure to Florida, I stood by Daniel's bed. He was just over a year old. I laid my hand on the little mound sleeping under the cover and prayed, "Oh, Jesus, he's yours. You care for him, Lord." I tiptoed into Dorothy's bedroom and prayed for her as she lay sleeping. I kissed Ofelia at the door, both of us choking back the tears.

"God bless you, Ofelia," I spoke quietly.

"God bless you, too, honey," she smiled. "I'll be praying for you. . . ."

I let go of her hand and strode away into the future.

Although the burden for Cuba was heavy on my heart, I felt the agony of being separated from Ofelia and the children. Were it not for the words of Jesus in Matthew 10:37-39, I would not have stuck with my decision and made the final flight. Jesus said,

He that loveth father or mother more than me is not worthy of me: and he that loveth son or daughter more than me is not worthy of me.

And he that taketh not his cross, and followeth after me, is not worthy of me.

He that findeth his life shall lose it: and he that loseth his life for my sake shall find it.

I love my family dearly. But in the light of God's great, all consuming sacrificial love, how could I do less than put Him first? His love covered me and my family; it also pushed me, moved me, lifted me to make this journey.

I was probably the only passenger on National Airlines to have seventeen extra pieces of luggage. After meeting Mel that evening in Orlando, we stayed one night with Ronald and Barbara Stansfield. That evening in their home, after we had finished reviewing the last-minute details of the trip, we prayed and shared God's Word with Ronald. One verse was, "No weapon formed against thee shall prosper." Another was in the section concerning the prophet Elijah, before whom the waters parted after he had slapped his mantle on the ground. The Stansfield family is a beautiful nucleus of faith and power in Christ Jesus. Their home is not a house but a church, and this was of great comfort to us.

Dawn broke gloriously the morning of May 26. As Mel and I lifted off the runway at Orlando International Airport in our Cherokee Six, the sky was clear. Our spirits echoed that of

the flight controller's voice over the radio, "A
beautiful day for Bimini! Have a good day, Eight
Zero Juliet."

Our flight would take us over Bimini, a tiny
island in the Bahamas, then to Nassau, Bahamas,
where we would land before beginning our
instrument crossover of Cuba to Montego Bay,
Jamaica.

In Nassau we received a bad weather report. A
storm was passing the area where we would be
flying. The exact location of the mass was not
known. It was not particularly severe, but it
could present a problem. Mel and I glanced at
each other without saying a word as the teletype
chattered in the background. The charts and
maps in the weather room presented a risky
situation. But how risky?

With no great drama, we simply continued
planning the flight. If we didn't go then, it
would take days to receive another clearance
from Cuba, and further complications could
arise. Downstairs Mel bought a T-shirt with the
slogan, "It's Better in the Bahamas." Compared
to where we would be flying, it *was* much better
in the Bahamas.

Once again we were on our way. It was warm
this May 26th evening when we left the runway
at Nassau. As Mel began a steady climb to
10,000 feet, I finished opening the seventeen
boxes of literature.

Night was falling as we approached the Cuban
coast and our fateful crossing through the Maya
air corridor. . . .

A tremendous clang of steel broke my fitful reverie. I sat up as the big metal bolt slid back and my cell door, a solid steel plate with a window flap, was opened. I was led downstairs to some tiny interrogation rooms. At every corner I would have to stop and face the wall, never seeing the face of another prisoner. My guard escort knocked, and I entered the cubicle and sat in front of a desk.

Behind it was a man with whom I would spend a few hundred hours—Captain Antonio Santos Salazar (probably not his real name). Looking very much in command with green uniform and silver stars, he sat composed, hands folded, smiling happily like a cat who has finally caught the mouse. Because of my fatigue, I remember little about that first conversation, except that he had been waiting a long time to catch me. When I was returned to Cell 44, still in somewhat of an emotional daze, I lay back on the bed, and again turned from side to side, trying to sleep.

Something caught in my hair, tickling my scalp. Reaching up to sweep away the supposed spider or cobweb, I felt a string dangling from the chain which held the bed. I sat up with a start, looking. There in the gloom of the cell, I found a cross which had been made from two mop strings twisted together. It was hanging by another mop string twisted with a human hair.

"A brother has been here before me. Praise God!" I breathed.

A mystical yet very real fellowship in Jesus

was now established. I was not alone! God cared. Others had walked the exact path which He was now having me walk. This was not simply an encouragement or reinforcement. It was a powerful spiritual bond between God, myself, and this other believer. Someday I will get to meet him.

A few hours later, after little sleep, I awoke as the one piece of hard white bread and "milk" was delivered. Eventually we learned that this milk comes in powdered form from China and is marked "for animal consumption only." Sometimes we suspected that drugs had been put into it.

As more light came through the window I began to explore. The window consisted of two slits formed in the concrete wall, making it impossible to see in or out. I noticed the word *Milagro*, which is Spanish for *miracle*, carved in the concrete on the lower slit. I wondered what sort of miracle might free me from here and thanked God for my still being alive.

For the first time, I noticed that the cell had four plank beds. Into the wood on the bed opposite mine was carved *Dios*—God. "Well, Lord," I said aloud, "You certainly do all things well." Not only did I have the mopstring sign of Jesus in my cell, but also carvings of God the Father and the Holy Spirit.

Shortly after my discovery, I was ordered out for another march to interrogation. As far as I knew, Mel had disappeared completely. I entered Santos' cubicle again. He was smiling and rubbing his hands together.

"Well, well, Thomas, I guess you know that your mission failed this time, huh? Yes, failed! You got away last year over Matanzas, but now here you are."

"Captain, although we crashed here, the mission didn't fail," I returned, looking him squarely in the eye. "You see, all of the literature was distributed. I really don't care what you do to me . . . are you going to shoot me?"

He laughed, shook his head and sputtered a "No." He was beginning a soft technique campaign.

"You CIA people always talk about poison pills and such things, but that's all drama . . . you never take them," he sneered. "You care too much. You're not going to die. And we aren't going to shoot you."

Santos held one of our tracts in his hand. I was delighted, for it was a gospel message written especially for him, a Marxist.

"But you realize that we will find all of this literature, don't you?" he blurted, seriously. "Why, our revolutionary people are voluntarily turning it in to the police. They're finding it on roof tops, in the streets, all over . . . but we will get it all."

(I learned later that this was a lie. The literature was well-received.)

"Should you confiscate it all, except for the one piece which you now hold, then my mission has not failed," I told him pointedly. "Just the fact that you are reading it is important to me.

If someday you alone allow God to enter your heart, then that would be worth my trip."

He seemed touched and puzzled by that. He read it again. Then, hiding behind his Marxist terminology, he called the paper a piece of "diversionism."

"Captain, you talk about peace, world peace. Let me ask you a question."

"Fine!" He smiled and leaned forward, hoping to draw me into conversation to subtly squeeze out information.

"The world is full of nations, right?" I began. "These nations have citizens living in states or provinces."

He knitted his eyebrows into a puzzled look and nodded.

"The states have cities. Cities have streets, and families live on these streets. So, the basic unit of government is the family, yes?"

He raised his hand in protest. "No. Communism is not family-oriented; it is a movement of the masses," he snorted.

"Captain Santos, do you fight with your wife?"

Amused by this personal reference, he relaxed, smiled, and sat back in the red vinyl chair. "Well, we have our disagreements, sure. Everybody does."

"Then," I pressed, "how can you talk about world peace when you don't even have it in your home? It has to start in your own heart."

"No, no!" He bolted upright furiously.

"Jesus can change society as He is allowed to

bring love and peace individually to hearts, to families, house by house from street to street. He gives me great peace even now as I sit here in front of you."

Suddenly the door burst open, and a major strutted into the room.

Regardless of his innermost thoughts, he was always listening or reviewing the tapes of my sessions with Santos. Every session was recorded. The major scowled at me.

"Stop this Jesus talk. You're with the CIA!" he yelled, waving both hands wildly.

I wanted to tell him that the army I represented was far greater in number, and infinitely more capable, than the CIA. The soldiers of Jesus use a weapon far more effective in this warfare, which is not of flesh and blood but against principalities, powers, and spiritual wickedness in high places. And that weapon is the powerful love of God. Instead, I was ordered back to my cell.

During the first few days, the feeling of total isolation which Santos tried to create was beginning to oppress me. "Your family thinks you are dead," he often told me. It was a lie, of course, because Mel's wife Mary had called the Coast Guard in Miami and learned that we were down in Cuba. "We can keep you here for years. No one knows about you."

As I lay back on my bed considering this, a wave of despair began to overwhelm me. Then I remembered that the Book of Revelation states that the names of those who have claimed Jesus are written in the Book of Life. With a loud voice I declared, "My name is in the Book of Life!" I felt a little of the burden lift. Without realizing it, I was swinging the sword of the Spirit, using the Word of God to defeat this devilish oppression.

Rising halfway out of the bed, I repeated over and over, "My name is written in the Book of Life." I didn't think through this spiritual concept, but it was working. That verbal statement was pushing darkness back, and I could feel strength beginning to flow through me. I jumped out of bed, raised my hands to God and cried, "Oh, thank You, dear God, thank You! They can do what they want with me because my name is there. I know my name is there."

The tears came in joy and release as He ministered to me. The praise and confession of His Word had broken one of the many chains with which Satan had wanted to bind me. The realization was exhilarating that I could not only remain "free" while in prison, but I could do something which, sadly, I rarely had time for before. I could learn to enjoy God and His presence.

5

Thírd Foot of the Cat

During those first easy days of interrogation, I began to pace up and down the ten-foot cell. Knowing the experiences of Christian friends who had been imprisoned for Christ in Romania, Bulgaria, and Russia in the last two years, I realized that my cell for four prisoners was immense. As I walked the five paces, I would repeat the names of Bible characters, recounting their circumstances.

"Daniel . . . two three four five. Rahab . . . two three four five. Shadrach . . . two three four five. Paul . . . two three four five."

I remembered Vasile Rascol, whose cell was so small that he developed vericose veins; Sabina Wurmbrand, who ate grass and fainted from weakness; and her husband, Richard, who for more than a year lay on a slab in a room for the dying.

I could hear the guards every weekend at their "church service" in the yard, chanting political slogans. Anyone who says that communism is not a religion has never lived in it. I am still amazed that our Bible schools and seminaries teach ways to witness to Buddhists and Hindus, but not to Marxists, who now constitute one of the largest "churches." I'm talking about a meticulously prepared doctrine of atheistic, dialetical materialism, which the faithful must place above wives, children, even their own lives. Is that not a "religion"?

The days passed. Santos, still smiling, would say, "Remember, you don't have to talk, but that light in your room will stay on all day and all night. How long do you want to wait? A year? No, it won't take that long. We'll be through with you before then."

That day as I lay on my bed thinking of his words, I heard someone whistling the *Star Spangled Banner.* I jumped up and put my ear to the hinge at the steel door. Perhaps it was a Cuban. Were there more Americans here? I whistled a few measures from the Marine Hymn and waited. A few seconds later floating down the hall came the other half! So there were more of us here. But the old phrase, "there is safety in numbers," didn't apply.

I had mentioned to Captain Santos about international laws against holding people without trial, but he would only laugh and say, "We don't have to obey any international law. Where do you think you are? This is Cuba."

Later, I met an American, Lester Perry, who had been held there ten years without trial. When Lester finally went to court, he was given a ten-year sentence. The following week, when the Communists learned that he had already been in prison for ten years, he was given one additional year.

Near the end of my first week, the captain—with a sense of drama—promised to show me something. The next morning, taking a small brown envelope from his pocket with a great flourish, he grinned, "I found something of yours. Remember, I promised I would have a little surprise for you?" He opened the envelope slowly and dumped the mop-string cross on the desk. Then with a triumphant smile, he sat back to study my reaction. I felt sorry for him. There was no power in the mop string or in a physical relic. The power is in Jesus, living in us fresh by the Holy Spirit each day.

"This cross is only a symbol," I tried to explain. "It's not important. Besides, I didn't make it; a brother in Christ did. But I did make another one yesterday, and it's hanging where you took that one."

His reaction surprised me. Santos sprang out of his chair as if it were an ejection seat, grabbed me, and almost ran back upstairs to my cell. Finding the other little cross, he jerked it off the bed, screaming, "The United States will pay thousands for this!"

His mind had locked into a fear-and-hate gear, carefully programmed for him by Marx and Lenin. Marx, the voice of the worker (who hardly worked a day in his life, but lived off other people), had called for the abolition of religion, referring to it as "the opiate of the people." But this screaming, glassy-eyed captain standing in front of me, crushing a little string cross in his fist, was showing me what ideological opium really was.

His frustration became more and more evident. Later during our conversation, I told him that God cares for our every need and how He can provide even in unusual circumstances for those who love Him. I mentioned Elijah the prophet, who was fed by the raven. The captain grunted and said nothing. As he led me to my cell that night, he screamed in front of the guards, "You're with the CIA, the CIA!" It seemed to me that he produced this little skit more to give himself courage than to intimidate me. He reached over to my bed and took away the tray of food.

The next morning in the interrogation room he leaned forward in his chair and sneered, "Well, did the little birds feed you last night?"

"No," I answered calmly, "but God gave me meat to eat that you don't know anything about."

This intrigued him, and he humored me as if I were crazy. I told him about the feast of love and joy that the Lord had brought to me in my room. I believe he was actually disappointed that no "miracle" had taken place. He was like a sad, hungry Herod. After one week, he tired of our spiritual conversations, which he regarded as an ideological merry-go-round, and began with increasing impatience to try to get on with the program.

"Did you know your face is turning yellow?" he would taunt. With a concerned look, he would study my face and talk about the cancer, which he said was growing again. I had no mirror.

"Look, Captain, I've probably had more psychology courses than you. You can't fool me with that cancer stuff," I scorned.

Throwing his arms back, he stood up and strutted toward me. His ego badly insulted, he raged about my white skin, how superior I felt to him, and accused me of bigotry.

"That's ridiculous! My wife is from Costa Rica, and my college roommates have been Africans," I countered in vain. He was using another hate division technique—race. He pushed a white button beside his desk, and the door in the back wall burst open. The short, muscle-bound major entered and began slamming his fist on the marbletop desk.

"You can't talk this way . . . this Jesus Christ . . . all this religion . . ." he screamed. "Where do you think you are, anyway? You think this is the regular police, huh? This is the G-2. G-2!"

He paused to wipe spittle off his lips. Pulling an object out of his pocket, he threw it on the

desk. I stared in wonder. It was a sea package—
the kind I had dumped in 1973.

"Thousands of these arrived on our beaches,"
the major shouted. "Why is the literature in this
package the same type you threw from the airplane?"

I didn't bother to answer him. What could I
say? Fascinated with this seven-year link, I
reached down and picked up the package,
touching a few grains of white sand along the
outside of the seam. He continued to scream,
trying to intimidate me by showing how much
they knew. I heard nothing. Inside I was
rejoicing. It had taken seven years to learn, but I
finally knew!

The angry Major Alvarez continued giving me
information. Many people had received the literature. The police also had found some. *Wonderful. They read it, too.* Although unsure that I
would ever see my loved ones again, I was con-
tent to know that the bread, God's bread, had
come back to me across the waters.

The major still wasn't finished. Evidently
seeing the look of pleasure on my face, he
opened the back door and motioned with his
finger. "Do you want to play baseball? I've got a
bat in the other room and some gloves. Come
on. Let's go play."

He was breathing heavily, and his eyes were
bloodshot. The baseball he referred to wasn't
exactly a game. I shook my head. On the way to
my room again, with Captain Santos, the same
accusations were hurled at me.

"You're a spy. CIA. Start talking or forget about seeing your family again," he spat.

Still, the little things were used by God to give me strength. Perhaps that is the way it is for those fortunate few who learn to be quiet inside and to notice their surroundings. I had much to learn. I could hear the birds. Such music! I remembered that the God who observes sparrows watches me.

Once I noticed a little white seashell embedded in the pink marble surface of the interrogator's desk. For two or three days I sat silently before Santos studying the seashell, while he faithfully went through his ideological rosary laced with taunts and threats. God's perfect architecture was marvelous and fascinating. How happy He must have been when creating this work of art!

Realizing he didn't have my attention one afternoon, the captain stopped his incantations and demanded, "What are you staring at?"

"The seashell."

The captain leaned forward to look, then raised his eyebrows as if to say, "So what?" Sitting on the edge of my hard wooden chair, hands folded as required, I talked to him softly.

"You see, I am so amazed at such a beautiful thing. The spirling curves within are so perfect. Such a matchless work of art. God has always been a sensitive architect."

The captain only grunted, grimacing at the little sermon.

"Perhaps," I continued, "God has a greater

appreciation and love for beauty than we do. Maybe He can place that beauty within us, too."

Santos shrugged his shoulders and acted unimpressed.

Before my interrogation the next day, the captain had another desk. The seashell was gone, but the Maker of the seashell was still there. I began to realize that, although I was not a brilliant ideological debater, nor an expert at explaining theology to an atheist, the Holy Spirit could use me at times in simple ways for His glory.

The captain was using his brand of logic, science, psychology and materialism, but I was tapped into the Creator of the universe. My responses were not brilliant, but they were given with love from my heart. Antonio Santos seemed to be weakening.

He tried a new method. The next few days Santos began using the names of my children to torment me. I had never given him their names, but evidently my family had been investigated in the United States.

"So, how is Daniel today? How is Dorothy?" Santos would grin, leaning back in his chair, hands folded behind his head.

He must have seen the pain reflected in my face. His new arrow pierced right through my heart.

"My children are in the hands of God." My voice almost broke. "I'll see them someday in Heaven."

"But you," Santos pressed home, "are in our hands. You won't see them again. What will they be like years from now? Growing up, alone, without their father?" He paused, watching the knives sink in. "Don't you think they might miss you?"

I can't describe the pain. I don't like to think about it. It was the worst day of my life.

I have heard that in other Communist prisons, Romania for instance, children have been placed in the cell next to a prisoner and whipped until they cry and scream. The desperate prisoner is told that they are his children. After watching Santos cruelly wield these names like a knife, I know this is possible.

Major Alvarez came in again. The officials were evidently being pressured from higher up to move faster with the interrogation process. I still didn't know if our families were aware that we were alive. Again screaming, the major commanded me to quit all of this Jesus stuff and start my CIA confession. But in his fury, he indirectly gave me more information.

"Do you think this is China? Do you think we can take the entire city of Manzanillo and lock them up?"

I smiled inwardly, realizing that Manzanillo had been talking about the "big hit on broadway" we had made in their town at 1:20 in the morning. It probably was the most excitement they had had in years.

I hoped that we wouldn't remain incognito for long, that our families would learn of our whereabouts. On one occasion a black plainclothes man, who they claimed was their superior, entered the interrogation room with the major. He blew cigar smoke in my face and stared at me.

"We're tired of playing with you," he warned coldly. "You think your religion is strong, but it's not. Our religion is three times stronger than yours."

After another round of futile questions, they left in disgust. Alone with me, the captain's attitude seemed to change.

"Have you ever lived in cold weather?" he questioned kindly.

"Yes," I answered, suspicious of this abrupt change.

"Do you like snow?"

"It can be fun."

"What kind of climate have you been living in?" he pressed.

"For the past eight to ten years, I've lived in the warm areas of the world."

He smiled and motioned for the guard to escort me back to Cell 44. This time my bed had been chained up against the wall. Lying on the floor, I sang a hymn with my head resting on my shoes.

"Stop singing!" the guard just outside the wall shouted.

I began to hum.

"Stop that, too!"

I whistled, "A Mighty Fortress Is Our God. . . ."

"If that's a hymn, you can't whistle, either," he stormed.

My captors were applying more pressure. About midnight my door was opened, and five big men strode in. One forced a thick black hood over my head and tied it around my neck. Was I going to be beaten? Terrified, I threw my arms in front of my chest and yelled, "I'll talk, I'll talk!"

I was led out of the building and thrown to the floor of a car. Two or three of the men sat in the back with their feet holding me to the floor. The handcuffs bit into my wrist. The car drove around and around the compound. The driver kept his foot on the clutch much of the time, revving up the motor to give me the impression that we were going to another prison. In later months I was to learn, from listening to sounds outside my window, that I was actually being taken back to the same building. This time the guards took me to a sealed-off section on the first floor where the police use their more refined techniques.

At first I was worried about suffocating, since there seemed to be no air inside the hood. The wire or string was tight around my neck. The car stopped and I was made to hop, jump, and crawl through the grass to get to another entrance. I heard a big steel door creak open as the men took me inside.

The first thing I became aware of in this section of the building was a tremendous roaring noise. I squatted, jumped, and crawled some more as the men drove me to another cell. They ripped the hood off and left me standing in the pitch black, cold room. Greatly relieved that I wasn't beaten, I stood there dazed, trying in vain to see. Then as my emotions and temperature cooled a little, I felt the cold coming in from over the door.

I stumbled over to it, put my hand up, and felt wind pouring out of a vent about three feet long and five inches wide. It was half-closed, with rags stuffed into it. My thin cotton, sleeveless coveralls didn't help much. Rubbing my arms, I explored the cell, finding a bed with broken springs and stinking mattress and an old wooden chair nailed to the floor.

"Well, this isn't bad," I mumbled. "At least I'm still in one piece."

I wondered why they didn't want to put marks on my body. *Maybe they have special reasons for everything they do.*

I lay down, but sleep was impossible in this cold. At times I have used the words "refrigerated" and "air-conditioned" in describing these rooms. Knowing my physical weakness and lack of sleep, I wondered how long I could stay alive in these rooms. The most precious thing I needed, and didn't have, was sleep. At the same time, Mother was praying for me in Texas that God would give me sleep. As usual, the Holy Spirit knows our deepest need. That day—June 7, 1979—Ofelia made a significant entry in her diary. The Lord had spoken to her, too.

Today I don't have beautiful enough words to thank the Lord for His goodness

to my husband. In these moments the Lord
is showing me His power, and I know that
He is helping my husband in a test which
he is now passing through. Hallelujah and
glory to God, for I know that He is going
to bring me my husband healed and safe,
and the glory will be for the Lord. Blessed
be the name of the Lord.

I can't believe that it is true, but it is a
reality that God works in each one of us in
such a way that we almost explode, full of
joy in any circumstance. Hallelujah.

Again and again Ofelia's faith reached across
the sea and into my ordeal. Again and again I
would be dragged and made to crawl and jump
to the interrogation sessions, always with the
hood over my head. I purposefully visualized in
front of me the great hand of God, a hand of
Light. I would see myself standing in the center
of this protecting and uplifting hand. Then I
would remember the secure promise of John
10:28, "And I give unto them eternal life; and
they shall never perish, neither shall any man
pluck them out of my hand." I was in God's
loving hand, no matter what they did to me.

I whispered this promise when I was placed in
a urinal, and when I was suspended over a supposed precipice.

The captain would smile when the hood was
torn off, sitting behind his desk in the little
room, which also was somewhat cool.

"It sure is warm today, isn't it?" he taunted, taking off his military jacket to begin the round of questions. "Who do you work for?"

"I work for Jesus."

"Oh, is that right? And how much money did this Jesus pay you for making these trips?"

"I took these trips for no pay. My pay is the love and blessing that God gives me for obeying Him."

Most of his questions centered around money, the CIA, and revolution. These were the only concepts of power that he seemed to understand. After about three or four days of cold and little sleep, I began to use a form of power which was new and unsettling to him. I was too tired now to even follow his train of thought. I sat in front of him, my head dropping, my thoughts wandering.

How can I fight this? This could go on for-ever. The Holy Spirit gave me a measure of pity and compassion for him, this man who was more in prison than I. I stopped responding to his questions and stared directly into his eyes. *Oh, God, help Antonio. Break through, Jesus. He is the one in the cold, for he has never felt the warmth of Your love.*

I continued to pray in front of him like this for hours. His questions came less frequently until he finally stopped.

"What are you doing?" he demanded.

"I'm praying for you."

His mouth dropped open. He ran one hand back through his hair, then rummaged for a cigarette. This was the first time I had seen him smoke. I continued to sit rigidly as he required, looking at him and praying.

He looked nervously around the room, then started drumming his fingers on the desk. In the next session I was surprised to see him wearing sunglasses. Evidently he didn't want me to see his eyes. God doesn't need eye contact. He deals with the heart. I continued praying.

Santos sent for Alvarez. The major was always his last resort. He stormed into the room, red-faced and angry as usual.

"So, you think this is a game?" he screamed, pounding on the desk for emphasis. "Now we are going to send you to see the third foot of the cat."

At times I could hear men screaming and pounding on the steel doors. It was hard to hear most sounds because of the tremendous roar of the blower and compressor which cooled this unit of the building.

I was thrown into another room. The hood came off and in a matter of seconds the heavy door slammed shut—a perfectly coordinated act which I feel sure had been done thousands of times in previous years. I was apprehensive about my new surroundings at first, but calmed down, thinking I was in the same room. Following the wall in the blackness, I discovered there was no bed or chair. In the first moments, as my body cooled from the exertions in the hall, I realized another difference. The blower vent over the door was fully open. The air was

pouring out at such a terrific rate that my hair
was blown straight out from my head.

I tried to walk in the pitch blackness to keep
warm, holding my hands out to keep from
bumping into the wall. But the wall was too cold
to touch. Besides, rather than warming me,
walking only brought me closer to the vent. I
huddled in the corner of the room.

"Oh God, help me!" I cried out in despair. He
would, only not in the way I wanted. I stuffed
the overalls into my socks to keep the air from
coming up my pants, then pulled my arms inside
the sleeveless top. I stretched the top up over
my nose so I could heat my body with my warm
breath. This would give me times of relief, but
then fatigue and slow but steady loss of body
heat would cause me to start shaking. I couldn't
bear to sit on the floor, nor lean on the wall.
The only easier position was standing with just
my forehead touching the wall.

Hours passed, and my feet and legs went
numb. I would stomp. When my feet swelled, I
would try to sit in a half squat with a small part
of my back touching the wall. Another day
passed. Mel was suffering up on the top floor
from the heat. Blisters and rashes, aggravated by
sweating, covered his body. I was covered with
dirt and urine and was losing weight rapidly
from the cold and lack of sleep. I had had no
bowel movements for nine days. A voice inside
me kept saying, "Go on, give up, it will be so
easy. Just take off all your clothes and lie down
in the center of the floor. It will take only a few

minutes. And the sleep will feel so good! You will be with God. Go ahead." Again and again the thoughts came.

"Oh, God, come and take me," I wailed. "I want to die. I want to die. I want to be with You, Jesus."

My spirit was still resting in Him, but my body and soul were agonizing. I prayed that the compressor unit and the blower would malfunction.

I thought about the CIA confession they wanted. *Well, they're only words. Fine, if that can get me out of this cold hell, then I'll play a joke on them.*

"I want to see the captain. I'm ready to talk," I yelled, pounding on the steel door. The guard rushed off, and a long hour later I was blindfolded and taken again to the interrogation room.

Santos looked pleased, sitting upright at his desk with a yellow legal pad and pen ready to write. It must have been late at night because he looked as if he had been in bed.

"You want a CIA confession?" I asked with pretended soberness. "Sure, I correspond with the CIA."

"You mean you receive mail directly from them?"

"Yeah, I get a check in the mail once a year for three million dollars."

I rubbed my arms to warm up a little, knowing that the joke wouldn't last long.

"What does the envelope look like? Does it

have an address on it?" Santos was beginning to look unhappy.

"I don't remember the address," I shrugged quite truthfully. "It just says Central Intelligence Agency in the corner."

Suddenly aware of my spoof, he slammed his pen down furiously. "You got me out of bed to tell me this?"

"You wanted a CIA confession, so I gave you one," I smirked.

He pressed a button, and this time helped the guard put the hood on. Back to the deep freeze. As the cell door slammed, I moaned, "No, no, no," and returned to my tropical corner which may have been one degree warmer.

I don't know why I remembered to sing. But God's hand was guiding and teaching. As the levels of punishment grew more severe, so did the intensity of spiritual warfare. Satan tried harder to drag me down, but God gently raised me up. Psalm 3:3 says He "is my glory and the lifter up of mine head." God was gracious, merciful and loving, asking only for a chance to prove Himself to me.

Again I started singing that great hymn, "A Mighty Fortress Is Our God." I sang "Jesus Loves Me," Bible choruses, and every Christian song I could remember. I was no longer conscious of the cold, only of Jesus. With eyes closed, my head barely touching the wall, I whistled, sang, even imitated a trumpet blasting out praises to the Lord.

Although I didn't think through the many

Scriptures which support it, I had entered the highest level of warfare against the enemy—praise. Psalm 22:3 says that God inhabits our praises. I don't know how this is accomplished, but it's true. The mighty Deliverer, the Messiah, the Savior was with me. He held my shaking body in His arms. I was with Jesus, no matter what happened.

Hypothermia, the gradual lowering of the body temperature, produces, among other things, confusion. The Bible says that God is not the author of confusion, that "God hath not given us the spirit of fear; but of power, and of love, and of a sound mind" (1 Timothy 1:7). The Holy Spirit within me was going to war on my behalf. The helmet of salvation was protecting my mind.

A guard opened the little steel window flap in my door and peered inside curiously.

"What are you doing?" he demanded.

"I'm singing about Jesus."

"Why?"

"Because I love Him," I replied happily.

He slammed the flap and left. I continued singing.

He returned a few minutes later and opened the window. "If you love Jesus, don't sing," he ordered, then left before I could reply. I felt so sorry for him, with his twisted, sad answer.

He brought the major outside the cell. Alvarez listened for awhile, then spoke in ominous tones, "Think, Thomas, Think!"

I cared nothing for his warning. I was enjoying angelic tones. His were harsh and empty, like the grating of nutmeg. He stormed away. At what I imagined to be three- or four-hour intervals, the window would be opened and a flashlight beam would snake across the floor searching for me. Finally, after perhaps two days and nights, I was taken out and placed in my former cell which, though cold, seemed warm in comparison. Convinced that I wasn't a super-spy trying to overthrow their country, the police were leading me back up the treatment ladder.

I spent another week in this cell, while they questioned me concerning my past seven years of activity over Cuba. Since I had planned the strategy and execution of these trips and had kept the work confined to an extremely tight circle of Christian friends, there wasn't much for them to learn. They kept probing for powerful government connections and sinister motives. Every shade and feeling of aggression and fear seemed to motivate them. This presented further opportunity to witness about the simple, clear, pure body of Christ, which works worldwide to fulfill the Great Commission.

Can the love and hope of Jesus be mixed with a condemnation of Marx-Leninism? In Acts 19:26, Paul was condemning the worship of the goddess Diana. He contended that she was not a god because she was made with human hands. He preached Christ as the only alternative.

Communism also is materialism, a worship of things made with human hands. Until the Marxist is awakened by the Spirit of God to see his condition and to thirst for the living water, he will hate the Church as an "oppressive" institution. There was a gospel for the Greeks, a gospel for the Romans, and a gospel for the Jews. It was all good news, it was all the same Jesus Christ. But each was tailored to fit the hatred or hunger of each group. For this reason I pressed the cause of Christ.

During the time spent in this "warmer" cold cell, I visited in prayer all the churches I had once attended. I began at Baton Rouge, Louisiana, the place of my birth. I traveled to Texas, Oklahoma, South Carolina, Grand Cayman, Costa Rica, Indiana, California. I sat with the believers and sang praises with them. I prayed for them and their pastors. I prayed for my parents and family in America, for the children and Ofelia, and her family in Costa Rica. I would walk five paces to each wall holding my hands out to keep from hitting it. I would take ten laps for each name as I spoke them to God in a whisper. Once when a guard opened the door, I noticed the clean path I had made across the dirty floor.

Finally, I was taken on the return journey in the car, only this time lying across the seat instead of the floor. When they lowered me into the back, I smashed my head on the edge of the door. After taking the hood off inside the building, two men carefully examined my forehead for a bruise. Because I hadn't been receiving humanitarian treatment, I was surprised at their detailed examination. I soon learned why.

6

Havana Tourist

W e want you to talk to our reporters," Captain Santos announced. "You see, we don't want to keep any American here twenty years. But first you must talk to our reporters."

I understood the not-so-subtle implication perfectly.

My skin was pale. He decided to prepare me for the press conference. I was shaved, given a toothbrush, soap, and a towel. The next day the guard motioned for me to follow.

"Come, go up for a little sun," he beckoned.

Sun? I hadn't seen sun or sky for about a month. I followed him up a narrow passage out onto a clay tile-inlaid roof. A concrete wall about ten-by-fifteen feet, topped with iron bars, was my cage where I would get sun whether I wanted it or not. (I learned later that Mel also was given the quick broil treatment.) The guard closed the door, and I looked up at the sky, squinting until my eyes adjusted to the light.

Six feet away I noticed some red markings on the wall. I still had poor vision without my glasses, but these letters were more than a foot tall. I read the Spanish: *Mi rey es Cristo.* I laugh with joy even now as I write it. *My king is Christ!* Another believer who had been on the roof before me had scrawled this with a piece of tile on the green concrete wall.

"Praise God!" I cried, throwing my hands up to Heaven before the Lord in worship and joy. The guard had asked me to come up for some sun, but again I would enjoy *The Son.* I was still having fellowship with the Church, the universal, undefeated, loving Church of God. I cannot express the joy and the tears of that moment.

I found other messages on the walls. *Sin Cristo no podemos ser nada* (without Christ we can do nothing). *Viva Dios* (Long live—or hooray for—God!), and *Jesus es la unica solu-cion, habla de el con tu corazon* (Jesus is the only solution; talk to Him with your heart). It was sheer Heaven. I studied those walls as scholars must have done the Dead Sea Scrolls. Here were messages of love and power to me from the living Church.

On my way back to my cell, I rejoiced at the fact that God was still leaving spiritual vitamins for me in miraculous ways. In future trips to the roof, whenever I would notice that the rain was washing His red clay messages away, I would take a piece of tile from the floor and reinforce the letters. I would add messages of my own, such as *Dios es amor* (God is love). In such a sick, starving environment, these simple truths were powerful medicine. This was theology enough.

In the following session, Captain Santos opened a large brown envelope and spread on the desk different Christian booklets and newsletters. He scowled disgustedly. "These pictures are false."

Pointing to a prison photo of Georgi Vins, he demanded, "How do they get these pictures?"

"Christians have cameras. There are lots of cameras," I replied firmly.

He became nervous at that statement, thinking of an army of spies. I was thinking of an army of love, a militia of light. A passage in Matthew passed slowly through my mind. It concerns the persecution of Christians.

Fear them not therefore: for there is nothing covered, that shall not be revealed; and hid, that shall not be known.

What I tell you in darkness, that speak ye in light: and what ye hear in the ear, that preach ye upon the housetops. And fear not them which kill the body, but are not able to kill the soul: but rather fear

him which is able to destroy both soul and
body in hell.

Matthew 10:26-28

I still had not seen Mel for more than a
month. He had been suffering in his small cell
from the heat, with a skin infection and a rash.
He, like myself, had dysentery. His interroga-
tions concerned Vietnam, racial prejudice,
politics and economics.

We finally saw each other on the night of July
3 as we arrived in separate cars at a television
studio in Havana. Neither of us had mirrors. He
said my skin was deathly pale and my eyes were
dark and sunken deeply into my head. He still
had some prison pallor in spite of sessions on
the broiler.

Mel also was threatened before the talk with
reporters. He was told that his future depended
on what he said. In reality, the reporters sitting
in the studio were G-2 police. We were going to
be taped and filmed concerning religious freedom in Cuba, though we had never seen a
church or talked to a citizen.

Sitting in soft chairs and wearing our street
clothes, we felt as if we were in another world.
We were even given glasses of cold water. But as
soon as the questions began, we realized that no
matter what face is presented, lies and hate look
the same, whether behind prison bars or in a
television studio.

The questions had been written out previously by our interrogators. The answers had been rehearsed with me many times, so there was no free exchange. Once, the United States was criticized as having a plastic society. Those who believe that ought to compare it with a Communist "canned" society. Plastic is a luxury.

Questions were asked over and over until two o'clock in the morning.

"Who paid you to make these trips?" asked a middle-aged man seated at the long table to our right.

"No one paid us," I replied.

"Wasn't your trip financed by some department in the United States government?" inquired a nicely-dressed young Negro woman beside him.

"No, it was paid for by Christians who love, who care."

The bright lights kept burning, cameras kept turning. Santos sat smiling in civilian clothes in the background, waiting for the "right" statements.

"But couldn't you have received funds, unknown by you, from some government organization?" the older man probed.

They still wanted to connect us to the CIA. I longed to throw them a bone, a verbal gift for an early release. My body cried out for freedom. The struggle was intense. I answered as diplomatically as possible, remembering threats of ice-water baths and twenty years in prison. We were given tea with lots of sugar to keep us going. Nonetheless, they were not satisfied with our answers. They stopped the interview and returned us to prison at interrogation headquarters.

On Sunday, July 8, we had a two-hour tour of the churches in Havana with the secret police. Again, we were in different cars and were rarely allowed to leave them. The "religious freedom" trip was poorly planned, if at all. I think God either confused the driver or managed to use the wrong one.

The first church was an enormous Catholic cathedral near the ocean in West Havana. Iron bars were welded across the windows and entrance. Eight- or nine-foot bars obstructed the sidewalk leading to the building. There was no gate in front. A side gate was opened after we had passed it and turned around.

"It must not be time for the Mass," Captain Santos observed with a straight face. Then he spoke angrily to the perplexed driver.

Mel's police guide in his car said the cathedral was open. Then the cars made a U-turn back to the "right" church. Six or seven people were inside, and a policeman across the street was watching them go in.

"Wow, the church is full!" Santos exclaimed excitedly.

Mel confirmed later that the church was nearly empty. We saw two more Catholic churches with about twenty people in each. One was a historical monument open for tourists, who were taking pictures.

We went to see a Baptist church, passing many prominent corner buildings with chained gates. All had stained glass windows, large entrance ways, and vaulted roofs. Were they churches? The Baptist sign had fallen off except for the missionary name of W. Carey. Again, we were not allowed out of our cars. I saw only two people in the building. Mel saw three. A stairway was built in the middle of the former sanctuary. During the "service" a woman entered the building with some sacks and walked up the stairs. It was an apartment house! The special tour was indeed poorly planned—but well-planned by God for our enlightenment. The captain was greatly embarrassed.

"It's big enough to be an apartment house," he smiled awkwardly.

Our cars were lost several times. The Adventist church was closed, naturally, since their services are held on Saturday. Metal plates were welded over the windows. A large lock was placed through the only opening on the door. I am thankful for Mel's extra sharp pilot's eyes. Without my glasses, I could see few of these finer details. We were told there were many Pentecostal churches all over Havana, but never saw one even though we were promised a look.

When Castro was asked in Jamaica why there were no new churches in Cuba, he said with his usual concerned, dramatic face that it was due to a lack of concrete. In fact, Cuba has so much

Because of government oppression, churches in Cuba are slowly deteriorating.

concrete that it is a major *exporter* to the Caribbean and much of South America.

On July 9, back in the television studio, we admitted to having seen some churches but we tried to be as non-committal as possible. I tried to interject various statements of faith but was cut short by the director.

"If you mention Jesus again, we will put your head under the ice," the major threatened at one point.

They wanted the taping to be strictly political. I mixed another "Jesus" into my answer but never saw the ice or frost. Mel said he believed that God had sent him on this mission. This made them angry. They definitely did not want this on their videotape and film. I felt at times as if I were in a vise. I had read for years of such pressure on Christians in Communist countries, but experiencing it was something new. Mel and I tried to please them in small ways without compromising, but this is impossible.

During the times of our taping, Captain Santos and other officials kept feeding me little statements such as, "When you get home . . ." and "Comb your hair so your wife will see you looking good," skillfully building false hopes. For a time I believed him. After returning to solitary, I would lie on the bed and fantasize, daydreaming about release, or escape. I pictured everything . . . the U.S. Marines landing on the roof . . . myself swimming across Havana harbor to grab a trailing cable from some ship. For a few days I fell into this trap, one just as deadly and habit-forming as drugs.

Finally, one day or night after another emotionally exhausting daydream session, I came to realize the total waste of time and energy involved. Asking the Lord's forgiveness, I developed a disciplined routine of walking two miles a day in the cell, singing, and reciting Bible verses aloud.

The verses would bless and strengthen me in a powerful way. Reciting, "I can do all things through Christ which strengtheneth me" (Philippians 4:13), I would pull out an imaginary sword and slash at the door with it. I was swing-

ing my sword of the Spirit—the mighty Word of
God. Oh, how I wished I had memorized more!
"Thy word have I hid in my heart that I might
not sin against thee," wrote David the Psalmist.
We in the free world need to hide it there for
many reasons, for our personal strength when
we aren't reading the Bible, and for the time
which may come when we can't *have* a Bible.

How I hungered for something to read! I read
all the scribblings on the walls. Some were by
Walter Clark, an American I met later in prison
who received a two-year sentence when his
plane, experiencing trouble, entered Cuban airspace. He and Bob Bennett were forced down by
MIGS. Walter, previously in Cell 37, had written
little love notes about his wife and children on
the door and walls.

Then one day Captain Santos, hoping to make
me a "Christian-Marxist" (such a thing does not
exist), gave me a book written by Padre Camilo
Torres, a Colombian priest. Torres preached
"love your neighbor" as a social concept only,
frustrated by what he felt to be a lack of
response in the established church. This social
gospel, no matter how well-dressed in spiritu-
ality, ends in ruin if not permeated with the
soul-saving, power-enduing love of Jesus Christ.

The supernatural transformation of the
human spirit by the power and grace of God
must be central and dominant or eventually
things will become distorted and twisted out of
shape. The seeds of Marxism planted in Torres
during his university years surfaced more and

more in his writings until the end. Father Torres died after advocating killing and organizing terrorists bands in the countryside. In the last chapters, the snake finally reared its ugly head, showing its true face. His teaching was not of simple economic or social change but that of hate, oppression and death.

But what a jewel I found in this book! Because of my poor eyesight, I had to place one hand over an eye so the other wouldn't tire too quickly. Holding the pages up to the dim yellow light, I found a passage of Scripture—Romans 8:35-39:

For who shall separate us from the love of Christ? shall tribulation, or distress, or persecution, or famine, or nakedness, or peril, or sword?

As it is written, For thy sake we are killed all the day long; we are accounted as sheep for the slaughter.

Nay, in all these things we are more than conquerors through him that loved us. For I am persuaded, that neither death, nor life, nor angels, nor principalities, nor powers, nor things present, nor things to come, nor height, nor depth, nor any other creature, shall be able to separate us from the love of God, which is in Christ Jesus our Lord.

What a feast I had! Torres was using the passage as a call to physical war and killing. But

the Holy Spirit ministered it to me in its true
perspective: that of the conquering love of
Christ in any circumstance.

Weak and again bearded, in ragged clothes,
completely cut off from all verbal forms of
communication with those who love me, I
allowed these rich verses to wash over me and
give me great comfort. The powerful chapter of
Romans 8 was written by Paul in prison: "Who
shall separate us from the love of Christ? . . .
tribulation . . . distress?"

Each day the captain would eagerly ask how I
was enjoying the book. He had gone to the
library himself to find it, still hoping to win me
to his side. I told him I was enjoying the book
immensely! I read through it once, then read the
passage from Romans seven or eight times a day.
I memorized the passage, but even then I would
open the book and touch the paper, marveling at
God's rich gift to me. I began to realize in a
small way how starved Christians are in Communist countries for the Word of God, and how
even a small portion of a verse can minister to
anyone, believer or non-believer.

In response to many official inquiries from
Washington and from members of Congress and
others, I was taken to a cancer hospital in
Havana for tests and X-rays. The captain used
this as an excuse to show me the "free" medical
treatment in Cuba.

I learned later that any item purchased in
Cuba—even such items as a pair of thin, poorly
made slacks—costs about a half month's wages. I

began to learn that here nothing is free. These poor people are indeed paying. All medicine must be purchased after the "free" treatment. Even low-grade vitamins cost a day's wages.

Upon arriving at the hospital, I waited in the car with a guard while the captain prepared what Mel and I remember as the "mango incident." I had once told Santos that I heard that, due to export, the Cuban people never got to enjoy their own mangoes. I learned that Bob Bennett's wife had to pay almost two days' Cuban wages for mangoes during a visit in Havana.

The captain finally came back to the Lada, a Russian Fiat, where we were waiting. Putting his hand on my shoulder, he led me slowly along the sidewalk. We were all wearing civilian clothes. I wondered why we were walking so slowly. Suddenly a woman who had just left the building came toward us. She carried a fishnet bag holding six or seven big, ripe mangoes.

This is getting interesting, I thought. *Let's see how he plays it.*

She walked by, and I believed for a moment that it was legitimate. But then, Captain Santos, the big dramatic hero, couldn't resist the opportunity to win an Oscar. With his hand still on my shoulder, he spun me halfway around. Pointing to the bag now passing us, he exclaimed, "Wow! Would you look at those mangoes!"

Beautiful, captain. You just executed a classic case of overkill.

The other guard with us also mentioned the fruit. Those were the only mangoes we ever saw during our several propaganda trips to Havana.

Later Mel and I were served in our separate cells. We were surprised to see fruit—mangoes! The guards were so amazed that they opened the steel flap in my door and asked me how I liked them. They did the same with Mel. We were learning that the Communists were masters of deceit, whether manipulating mangoes or multitudes of people.

Not only is fruit scarce, but dozens of necessities have to be rationed. The ration book is a present day reality and grim reminder of the poor economy. Many blame the U.S. embargo for Cuban poverty. It is rather the Communist system that strips the people. In the sixties, Fidel the "economic expert" lost millions of pesos on disastrous experiments.

His rabbit plan—all the imported rabbits died, unused to the tropical heat.

The pig plan—a cold weather type pig brought from the north had to be kept in specially built air-conditioned huts to survive. The air conditioners broke down. The pigs died.

Castro wanted coffee trees grown in a semicircle around Havana after the leading British expert said it was impossible. All the trees died.

The frog plan. The crocodile plan.

Finally the Russians, seeing millions of rubles-pesos being poured down the drain, placed Soviet advisers in every department of government. Still the sad situation is reflected by political cartoons, which began mysteriously appearing on city walls during my time there: A horse is collapsing on the ground in front of a heavy cart. The caption reads, "Don't push us anymore; we are almost on the ground."

Suffering and pain are so prevalent in Communist countries that dozens of jokes usually emerge as a result. I always found it amazing that the telling of such jokes would evoke genuine laughter. There is a popular joke which accurately reflects the economy: Fidel wanted to improve his security force, so he hired Sherlock Holmes, the famous detective, to advise him. Sherlock rode with Fidel in his jeep for several weeks, saying nothing.

"Look, Sherlock," said Fidel, "I know you're famous and all that, but you aren't helping me a bit. Why don't you give me some hints?"

Sherlock pointed up to the tenth floor of an apartment building. "You see the man with the new red shirt? He's not wearing any underwear," Holmes stated wisely.

Castro immediately dispatched his G-2, who threw the surprised man against the wall and lowered his pants. Sure enough, no underwear.

"I'm sorry, Sherlock," Fidel apologized. "It's all true. You are worth every cent I am paying you. But tell me, how did you know? It's incredible! You know every detail."

Sherlock smiled. "Well, it's elementary, my dear Fidel. You see, according to the ration book, your citizens can only receive one new shirt or one new undergarment per year. I saw that he had the new shirt, so I knew he couldn't be wearing the underwear."

Now came a period of waiting. For nearly two months we sat in our separate cells. The eyes and the spirit hunger for so many things when they are absent, things we take so much for granted. Color. When we had passed flowers by the roadside, I held my breath, drinking in the living vibrant pinks and reds, looking at them every possible second so as to remember them later. In the cell there was no color.

Once I climbed up the door by putting my toes on some welded joints and found some dead lacewing insects in a small pocket under the lightbulb. I held the tiny, fragile, iridescent wings under the light, looking at the beautiful greens and pinks. My breath knocked them out of my hand to the floor. I climbed down, getting on my knees to look for them but, with no glasses and poor light, it was useless.

I wondered how long this ordeal would continue, and when—or whether—I would ever see Ofelia and the children again. Although the presence of the Lord was ever near, the waiting seemed endless.

7

"Internal Security"

The long, hot days and nights of July and August passed slowly. Pacing in my cell for exercise, I paused and slapped my towel on the bed, remembering Elijah parting the water with his mantle.

"So God will do for me someday," I claimed out loud.

Confident that He would one day part these steel doors, I relaxed and dropped bread crumbs outside for the birds. They encouraged me with their songs of praise. A little brown bird with an orange beak poked his beak through my window slit, tilting his head sideways to look at me. I remembered one night at Gulf Coast Bible College in Houston, Texas: My alarm clock didn't work, and I asked God to help me to awaken the next morning at six o'clock. In the morning a "bang! bang! bang!" aroused me from my sound sleep. Getting out of bed, I saw on the brick ledge outside a sparrow hammering on the glass with his beak. It was exactly six o'clock.

Though the frequent bouts of dysentery kept me in a weakened state, I continued to pace the cell. I knew when Sunday rolled around because the guards would chant in unison to Fidel, Che, Camilo, and other gods outside the building. Hour after hour they chanted poems, songs and slogans.

During the time our milk was distributed, I tried to talk with the guards. A young one would laugh and say, "Why do you talk of this God? Fidel Castro is our god." Another who brought the food every day would pause in front of the door for a few seconds. I would smile and say, "Jesus bless you." He would smile back and say nothing. On one occasion, when Captain Santos was in my cell, this young guard came by with my food. Occupied with the interrogation, I couldn't give him my quick blessing. A few minutes later he returned and peeked inside.

"Hey! Where is my 'Jesus bless you'?" he grinned.

With a stunned look on his face, the captain whirled toward the door, but the guard was gone.

To fight the boredom, I increased my walking to three miles a day. Pacing back and forth, I recited aloud all of the names of Jesus that I could remember: "Emmanuel (God is with us),

Savior, Master, King, Lord, Rock. . . ." Jesus as the Rock was the spiritual concept which most powerfully nourished my soul and gave me strength. I had no material possessions, no family, and definitely no respect from my peers, but I did have the Rock. I was learning daily to stand on Him.

The name of this interrogation prison was Internal Security. I laughed at the irony, for within my heart seeds of faith were budding. I was growing because of His grace and He was building within me more internal security than I had ever known before.

Below, on the first floor, the captain was still trying to destroy that security. His efforts at picking apart my belief in God were relentless. But the more I referred to the Rock—and to His sacrificial love—the more difficulty Santos encountered in his chipping technique. He could try to hammer away at the "outwardly religious" Tom White, but he couldn't touch the mighty Cornerstone, the living Jesus within.

In my cell I had much time to reflect on the anti-God philosophy that permeates every facet of Castro's society. Here, in part, is why the Church in Cuba suffers. Not only has this Marxist religion served to oppress the Church, but it gnaws away at it from the inside like a cancer.

A generation of new pastors now praises Marx, Lenin, and Castro as Messiahs. Lenin had said, "We must fight religion. This is the ABC of the whole of materialism and consequently of Marxism." What has developed in Cuba reflects

Solzhenitsyn's statement in 1972: "A church led by athiests—a spectacle which man has not experienced for 2,000 years!"

Monsignor Zacchi, the papal nuncio in Cuba, has said that Catholic youth may become members of the Communist Youth Organization because Catholics have a right to be politically involved. Some priests privately and sadly disagree with him.

The head of the Union Seminary in Matanzas is Reverend Sergio Arce. He has grown a full beard in honor of Castro—Castro the Bible burner.[1] Arce recently commented, "Marx was an atheist in his head but not in his heart. Too many Christians are not atheists in their head but are in their hearts."

At first glance this appears to be an endorsement of a kind, gentle Marx, who wanted the poor to have a better living. The Christian is depicted as a selfish, gluttonous materialist, loving others in word only. Much of the naive western world is being drawn into this erroneous comparison, and they remain silent. They are made to feel like "economic criminals." But the true Christian loves and gives and helps and sacrifices, as shown by Christ's example.

What was Marx's example? We know what was in Christ's heart. But what about Marx? Was he really a benevolent humanitarian economist?

Marx the economist also was Marx the poet. His poetry and economics are interwoven. In his

---

[1]Quoted by Janice Barfield, *You Can Fly* (Grand Rapids: Zondervan, 1981), 119.

poem "Human Pride," he reflects what his plans will actually do to the world, and his poetic prophecy is being fulfilled as Marxist countries are economically raped.

Human Pride

With disdain I will throw my gauntlet
Full in the face of the world
And see the collapse of this pygmy giant
Whose fall will not stifle my ardour.

Then will I wander godlike and victorious
Through the ruins of the world
And, giving my words an active force,
I will feel equal to the Creator.

Why does Marx equate himself with the Creator? What has this to do with economy? In Marx's poem "The Player," he writes:

The hellish vapors rise and fill the brain
Till I go mad and my heart is utterly changed.
See this sword?
The prince of darkness
Sold it to me.

In his poem "The Pale Maiden," he admits:

Thus heaven I've forfeited,
I know it full well

My soul, once true to God
Is chosen for hell.

In a letter dated March 31, 1854, Marx's own
son, Edgar, addressed his father as "my dear
devil." [2] Are Marx's economic theories—which
may appear attractive to the poor of the world—
in reality disguised as "angels of light"? Do they
not open the lid to a Pandora's box of economic, moral, and spiritual slavery? And do not
the Marxist priests of G-2—Antonio Santos,
Major Alvarez, and others—perfectly fit the true
mold which these theories helped to create: not
benevolent saviors aiding the poor, but vicious,
atheistic oppressors, open mockers of God,
aggressive destroyers of Christian life and ethics?
Why is it that, among all governments which
publicly declare themselves Marxist, religious
oppression abounds?

The oppression of communism is apparent
not only in the economic and political arenas,
but in the very spirit of Cuban life. Suspicion
and fear are weapons of control.

Knowing that separation from my family was
an open wound to me, the officials continually
used their names to tempt and torment me. The
deep agony of their tactics became unbearable,

---

[2] Documentation of this dark, little known facet of
Marx's life, reflected in his letters, poems and other
writings, can be found in *Was Karl Marx a Satanist?* by
Richard Wurmbrand.

twisting and churning my spirit each passing day.

"Oh, God! I can't get rid of this . . . this pain. . . . It's too strong. Help me!" I wept pleadingly one evening. Daniel, with his golden hair, splashing gleefully in the bathtub, was in my thoughts. I envisioned Dorothy clapping her hands and singing little choruses. Then there was Ofelia—how I ached for her—caring for them, alone.

Rolling from side to side on my hard bed, I was startled by a thought that flashed into my troubled mind.

"Tom . . . remember the centurion!"

The impression was so strong it couldn't have been more clear if I had heard it audibly. I sat up on the edge of the bed, perplexed.

"What does that have to do with the problem?" I whispered. "The centurion?"

"Tom, remember the centurion. Think about it," the command came again.

My mind raced to Luke, chapter seven, where Jesus marveled at the centurion's faith. The Roman soldier was the first person who believed that Jesus could care for a problem in his home, without physically being there. As this realization began to dawn, a smile played across my lips.

"Then You, Jesus, can go in the Spirit right *now*, from here in my cell in Havana to my home in Glendale, California. You now can touch my wife and children. You can be with them at this very moment. Oh, praise God! Go there now, Jesus."

It was a simple lesson . . . a little piece of
meat for a baby Christian who rarely put the
Scripture to work. This meat was a faith builder.
It was thrilling. God had given it to me, just for
my problem, in a personal package. Feelings of
sadness for my family would still come over me,
but never again the agonizing tormenting oppression. When Satan would try to stab me, I would
swing my sword back at him and say aloud,
"Remember the centurion!"

Encouraged by this victory, I began repeating
Bible verses, singing more Scripture choruses,
hymns, and praises every day. As I came closer
to the feet of Jesus, an awareness of my weaknesses and problems grew. Things which are so
easily hidden in a busy, distractive society
bubbled to the surface during my time of prayer
and fasting with the Lord. My cell had become a
"prayer closet."

I learned that Jesus my Creator is the greatest
psychiatrist who ever lived. He does not simply
solve problems, He "dissolves" them in His
blood. As each problem came to light, I would
visualize a golden cross over them. This served as
a reminder that my weaknesses had no more
hold over me. I began to feel free, washed,
squeaky clean, fresh.

A prophecy about Jesus in Malachi 3:2 took
on new meaning for me: ". . . he is like a
refiner's fire, and like fullers' soap." A tiny piece
of white soap across from my bed made me

chuckle. Free. Clean. Jesus was washing His baby.

How often I have rushed around leaving no time for a "wash job," running into church on Sunday the way we make a quick visit to a car-wash. Jesus finally had a "captive audience," and He was giving me a thorough heart-wash.

I was overjoyed to know that He still cared for me. Many nights I had rolled on the bed, praying, "Oh, God, don't cut me off." I remembered that the branch which doesn't bear fruit is cut off. I could have borne more fruit for Him. Was I cut off now? His sweet, loving ministry to me those days and nights was encouraging. He still loved. He still cared. He even prepared.

In December 1978 I was praying at a home prayer meeting with some Christian friends. One who knew of the work I was doing suggested that the group pray for me and my missionary work. After the meeting, a woman revealed something which the Lord showed her.

"While praying for you, I saw you hurtling down a highway in a tank-like object. But don't be afraid because angels were sitting on your left and right. Nothing can harm you."

I murmured a thanks to her for the information, wondering what sort of prophecy this might be, if it were indeed a prophecy. In the Book of Acts, a man named Agabus predicts Paul's imprisonment in much the same way. But that was for the days of the Apostles, wasn't it? Besides, I was using an airplane. What could this tank-like object be?

Sitting in my solitary cell thinking about the woman's statement, I remembered the airplane hitting the garbage truck. With the wings breaking off and the fuselage hurtling down the highway, the airplane had become a tank-like object. No scratches on our bodies. "Nothing can harm you." "Angels." Yes, God not only cared, He prepared. God was behind me and before me.

In late August, before our move to the main prison, Captain Santos had a fatherly session with me. Playing the role of a wise sage, he advised me to stay out of politics and keep to the "pure religion." This amused me. Here I was listening to the same words I had heard from heads of denominations, religious officials, and other clergy who criticized Bible smuggling—yet this identical sermon now came from a Communist captain who had treated me coldly, brutally, like an insect: "You shouldn't mix politics with the gospel. You should just preach the pure gospel."

Santos had admitted to questioning priests and pastors of various faiths. In what type of politics were they involved? Were they the politics of "My King is Christ," which I had seen on the wall? Were they the politics of the mop-string cross? I would soon find out. I was about to meet some of these "politicians," my brothers in Christ.

8

In the School of Sufferology

S oon Mel and I were transferred to another prison in a Russian van similar to the "Black Marias" I had seen in films of Soviet labor camps. It was night. Matt, another American, and we chattered happily together in the back, speech running over like a waterfall in joy of communication. We must have seemed like songbirds in a cage to the three or four guards who sat on the other side of our own wire cage. They all carried machine guns (AKM assault rifles), Soviet guns with Russian bullets. Why night-time? Why so many guards? We were unused to such a tremendous show of force.

This was the beginning of our education concerning the police state. These were special guards of the Ministry of the Interior. There also are guards and soldiers of The National Revolutionary Militia, National Revolutionary Police, Territorial Militia, and three separate armies of the Ministry of the Armed Forces—all created to maintain total control over the people.

We entered through the main gates of Combinado del Este prison east of Havana. Though we couldn't see through the window slits of the van, we could hear the bee-like hum of thousands of voices—seven thousand, it turned out. We were taken to building three and placed in a temporary holding cell. The cells were packed. In our cubicle twenty-eight *launcheros* were sleeping on the concrete floor. They had been sentenced to four years in prison for trying to leave Cuba illegally on inner tubes, boats and rafts.

One told me how his five-year-old daughter rode on his lap in an inner tube as he rowed forty miles out to sea toward Key West. The Cuban torpedo boats not only leave Castro's waters but patrol almost to the United States boundary, fishing for escaping countrymen. Mel, Matt, and I were given the only bed. They felt honored that we were there.

I sat on top of the bunk and looked at them. Knowing that I could speak Spanish, they had all crowded around, eager to talk. Thin, unshaven, dark hollow eyes, missing teeth, ragged clothes or little clothes at all—their tropical paradise was a living hell. What could I say?

"I sure would like to escape with you!" I exclaimed quite truthfully. "How far is the beach?"

"About three miles north," one laughed.

"Even when you escape did you know that there is something which you can never leave behind?—yourself. Your problems. Your personality. I know someone who has given me real freedom," I paused, waiting for my words to sink in.

They stared at me questioningly. One old man put his hand to his whiskered chin.

"Jesus Christ! He makes me free," I continued. "He takes off all the tired, dirty things which would try to pull me down."

I didn't see one scornful face among them. Many cried. They crowded around the bunk looking like tiny fish coming to the surface of the water, mouths open for food. Some were mere skeletons.

I stepped down from the bed and stood with them. Slapping my hand on my chest for emphasis I claimed, "I am just as free standing here with you, right now, as I would be in Miami Beach. The liberty that Jesus gives can never be taken from you." They were getting excited.

"Do you know the Bible?" one asked. "Give us some words from the Bible," another implored.

I felt embarrassed. God, why hadn't I memorized more Scripture? I began with the Beautitudes. "Blessed are the poor in spirit . . . Blessed are they that mourn: for they shall be comforted. . . ."

I taught them a gospel chorus which Ofelia

had learned in Costa Rica: "The name of Jesus is sweet; He brings me peace and joy." They sang timidly at first, then a little louder. Some clapped.

The thinnest among the prisoners was a young man of eighteen who came to me many times, saying, "Tell me more. All I have is this poison in my head ever since I was a baby." He told me about the poison: Marxism, dialetical material- ism, atheism. I would quote in Spanish the Twenty-third Psalm and other verses about the love of God. I explained to him and the others how easy it is to talk to God.

"God is present with us in this room right now. You don't need special words. You talk to Him like you would to your friend. His Son, Jesus, carries your words directly to Him. He loves you."

He would become so happy, we could see him being filled. I gave him my breakfast of Chinese animal milk, which was no great sacrifice for me but was precious to him.

The next night we saw a few men die in holding cells from asthma and weakness. For hours their fellow prisoners had called for help. Their bodies were unceremoniously carried out. According to Marx, they are only material, so why create a fuss?

Our heads were shaved, we filled out forms, we were finger-printed, and given prison uni- forms. After three months in Cuba under inter- rogation, we were now processed into prison. No lawyer, no trial, no letters. I remembered how

Captain Santos had laughed when I asked him about international law. "This is Cuba. Cuba! *We* are the law. We respect no international law."

Transferred from building three to building one, we left the *launcheros.* I would meet them again under tragic circumstances.

Next to the prison we saw the factory where steel and concrete forms are made for more prisons. This labor is done by prisoners, a sort of perpetual motion machine, more slaves to build more prisons for more slaves. We could see huge new prison complexes being erected in the hills around us. The long factory can be seen to the left of the prison in the photo. Every morning and evening long grey lines of tired men form in front of building one and walk to the factory like a great grey centipede, their countless moving legs having almost a hypnotic uniformity.

We entered the international wing and met Americans, Frenchmen, Africans, Dutch, Colombians, and Englishmen. Some had common offenses, some had their boats or planes seized. Others were there for voicing opinions that differed with those of the State.

I was first amazed at the cleanliness and nice appearance of the prison, with its outside basketball courts, visitor's center, and hospital. Perhaps this system had some humane tendencies after all. That was outside. Inside, the building was cockroach city. Hundreds of huge rats scampered rampant in and out of the building.

Seven hundred cases of venereal disease were

Combinado del Este Prison

1. Concrete factory where prison labor makes more prisons.
2. Headquarters for prison officials
3. Two of the main cell blocks. The Americans spent equal time in both buildings.

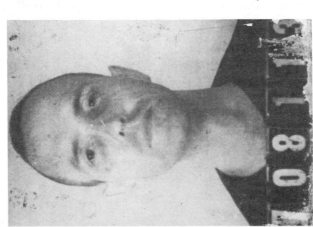

This official prison photo of Tom White was smuggled out several months before his release.

in our facility alone. The doctors, prisoners themselves, told me about the epidemic. Yet the World Health Organization reported that Cuba only had thirty-six cases. Gullible officials of other countries hail Fidel and his great medical advances, but no one asks where the WHO obtained its figures or who released them. The Minister of Health in Cuba also is the Minister of Education, the Minister of Culture, and the Commander-in-chief of the Army—Fidel Castro.

In the following months we continued to learn that Combinado del Este is a "show prison." All foreign delegations who are interested in seeing the prison system are taken in scenic-cruiser buses through the streets. Prisoners in special basketball uniforms are playing outside. All political prisoners or others considered vociferous are denied hospital visits or movement as the buses drive slowly by for the big show. When the delegations leave, the basketball show disappears.

A reporter once was on our floor, but we were not allowed to talk to her. Hours before her arrival the compound was sprayed with a heavy dose of bug killer. Solzhenitsyn tells an anecdote about Eleanor Roosevelt's similar visit to a model Soviet prison. The circumstances and deception have not changed.

The Communists have learned through careful study that most of the West wants to believe its deception. It's troublesome to believe the negative and comfortable to embrace the positive. So they gladly accommodate with a carefully planned, artfully designed cosmetic mask. The statement, "You can't fool all the people all the time" applies to the residents, but not to the visitors of the people. The religious delegations and study groups that pass through Cuba are treated to an enlarged version of our "mango incident."

On our first day with the Americans, we met Glenn Akam. Glenn's plane had crashed in Cuba two years earlier. I was thrilled to notice that he had some Christian literature and eagerly began reading it, holding it closely to my face. When would I ever get new glasses? The Cubans' Christian literature was confiscated when found. For awhile we foreigners were allowed to read freely. As I read the gospel tracts and booklets with joy and hunger, I once again realized what it means not to have this food available.

We learned that some Cuban Christians and political prisoners lived on the fourth floor. One morning I heard them singing; thirty or forty male voices powerfully penetrated the sordid prison atmosphere. They were singing of victory, of love, of hope—of Jesus. Immediately I wanted to go to the fourth floor. My brothers were there. My family. I had heard that a pastor was there among other believers.

Mel and I had listened at the stairwell to Everett Jackson, an American who lived on top with some of them. "Hey, pilgrims, the guys up here really want to meet you," Everett yelled down to us. We wondered how they knew we had come to Cuba. They seemed to know all about our literature and our flights.

There was an elevator which carries food up to the floors and brings garbage down. I stepped into it, trying not to slide on the grease and filth. The prison workers closed the grate as I squatted, hiding behind the barrels. The lift rattled and creaked upward to stop at the fourth floor.

"It's the American!" one exclaimed as he helped me out. Prisoners did all the work. "Quick, stand over here."

I stood by the wall as he looked for the guard.

"You can't come up this way anymore!" he exclaimed cautiously.

"Why not?" I shot back.

"The cable has broken twice; you could be killed! When the time comes for another visit, we'll find a way to move you."

I turned and watched the creaking elevator descend down the long shaft. "Do you know where Pastor Noble's cell is?" I asked.

They all smiled. Lara, Tony, Luis, Leon . . . they had all lived together with Noble in prison for nearly twenty years now. Yes, they knew where to find him.

There were always guards, but with silent hand signals and prisoners stationed at certain locations, I was usually able to move around as I pleased. I prayed as I ran past certain check points until I met my brother, a short muscular black man with a smile like sunshine—Reverend

At left, Nobel Alexander before his arrest in 1962. Prison sketch, drawn in December 1975, was smuggled to his family. He is still in captivity.

Noble Alexander. Noble was imprisoned for preaching in Matanzas about original sin. The Communists took offense at that sermon, declaring that this implied that they were sinners, too.

Noble is an unusual pastor. He has hands like steel and thick fingers, but he can make a shirt from a bedsheet with stitches so fine that they are almost invisible. His back is scarred with rifle-bullet fragments and chips of concrete. While in La Cabaña prison, he would have a prayer circle. The guards would fire into the middle of the circle to disrupt the service. Most of the men would not move, but continued to sing and pray while the shrapnel was embedded in their flesh.

"Sometimes one of us would break the circle and just run," Noble laughed, "but he would come back. They would beat us and beat us." He smiled as if enjoying a private joke. I learned that it wasn't a joke at all—it was a private joy. Noble's back may be scarred, but his spirit isn't. He gives half of his food to the older or weaker prisoners.

"Why are we being called pilgrims, and how did everyone know about our literature?" I asked Noble one day.

"We have been reading your tracts," he explained happily. "The first week in June some were passed into the prison. We all read them."

The first week in June was only a few days after we had crashed in Manzanillo. The literature was dropped in Camaguey province more than two hundred miles from the prison! If it was smuggled into the prison such a long distance away, how was it being received in the towns where we had dropped it? We would learn more. We were in Cuba to learn. We were in God's school.

Noble taught me much more, not with words, but with his example of sacrifice mingled with joy. During his eighteen years in prison, he and other Christians have been enrolled in the rich, rewarding school of sufferology. The Apostle Paul speaks of "the fellowship of His sufferings" in Philippians 3:10.

Sufferology, martyrdom, pain, and oppression among the brotherhood are courses never taught in schools of theology. God Himself teaches these classes, graciously inviting us to attend, never forcing us. When we avoid them, we miss priceless fellowship and settle for cheap, comfortable substitutes.

Through the prison grapevine to the street, and from more inquiries from Washington, U.S. officials in Havana learned that we were being held at Combinado del Este. Appeals were made to the Cuban government that we be permitted visitors.

In September I had a three-hour visit from my parents. Mother brought me some glasses, not knowing but suspecting that I needed them. Once again the Holy Spirit had streamlined things. Ofelia and the children were fine. She was quiet, calm and trusting the Lord. We had a monthly visit from the U.S. Interests section for about twenty minutes. So the word was out. People knew about us. More than a hundred official inquiries had been made to the State Department about us.

9

Counter-Revolutionary for Christ

O n the 25th of October we finally went to trial—five months after we had crashed. Little concept of time exists in the judicial system of Cuba. The law books mention trial before 180 days imprisonment. We met Americans and hundreds of Cubans who had been waiting years for their day in court.

Taken in another Russian prison van, we arrived at downtown Havana and were escorted into the courtroom. The fact that I had had some weak moments at the television studio haunted me. Now another test had come. Can a Christian move in faith and still "feel" fearful? Paul Tournier has written, "The adventurous life is not one exempt from fear, but on the contrary one that is lived in full knowledge of fears of all

kinds, one in which we go forward in spite of
our fears."[1]

Would I be able to pass this test? As we were
seated on a long bench at the front of the room,
I felt a surge of power. Regardless of the consequences, I resolved to speak boldly the words
God would give me.

Our lady lawyer, whom we had not met,
walked over to Captain Santos and straightened
his tie and coat.

"Antonio! How are you? You sure are looking good!" she greeted him affectionately.

A guard held a Russian AKM assault rifle to
our backs. I really wasn't too amazed by the
circumstances. Many of my Christian friends
from Romania, Bulgaria, and Russia had described similar ordeals. The trials were a sham,
set up previously by the security police organs.

The five black-robed judges entered the room.
We sat, and our lawyer presented our defense.
Her interrogation consisted of four questions:
"How old are you? Are you married? Do you
have children? What is your occupation?" That
was our defense. Then Captain Santos came forward to present his story. He pulled my old
plane tickets and papers out of his pockets with
a flourish. Standing slightly in front of us and to
our left, he swiveled from time to time, gestur-
ing in our direction dramatically.

"Dedicated to penetrating our air space for

---

[1]Quoted by Janice Barfield, *You Can Fly* (Grand Rapids:
Zondervan, 1981), 119.

seven years," he shouted. Never once mentioning Christ or religion, he claimed that we were flying as "counter-revolutionaries."

"1973 . . . boat trip . . . thousands of pamphlets . . ." On and on he ranted in a high-pitched voice. The guard behind us with the rifle uttered different expressions of amazement. This was a real show for him, a private screening, featuring the Americans who "threatened the stability and security of the State."

I had the strongest feeling that Santos was not the performer but the conductor of the trial, waving an ideological baton behind his back. The courtroom was his. The judges were his. He was the vanguard of the holy Marxist faith.

Santos took most of the time. Two of the five judges slept. Only one in the middle seemed to be really paying attention. Now the prosecutor wanted to question us. I was called first. I walked up and stood in front of him with an interpreter by my side. Disregarding him most of the time, I exchanged thrusts in Spanish directly with the prosecutor.

"The literature we dropped was not an attempt to overthrow the government, but was a presentation of life after death," I shot.

"How do you know there is life after death?" he pressed scornfully.

"We can't see it, but we believe it by faith; someday we all will know the answer." I looked him squarely in the eye then added, "You will, too!"

He pushed his glasses up on his nose. "Don't

you realize that you two are the only fanatics in
this court who believe like this?" he sneered.

"Not really," I shot back. "There are thousands in this room standing here right now who
believe as we do."

In mock surprise he looked around the room
for the thousands.

"The saints and angels are in this room; God
is here. There are many witnesses here," I
pressed my point further.

Our lawyer appeared nervous and sad. She
began picking at her fingernail polish, head
down, hardly daring to look up. I felt sorry for
her.

"What is a saint? I have never seen one," the
prosecutor continued sarcastically, hoping to
catch me off guard.

"You're looking at one."

His mouth dropped open and he sat back in
his chair.

"You see," I interjected, "when a person is a
believer in Jesus Christ, the Bible calls him a
saint."

During my discussion with him, I noticed that
he was holding a piece of literature. It appeared
to be what we had dropped. None of the judges
had one. Neither did our lawyer. Thinking that
perhaps there was at least one scrap of justice in
this paper maché ceremony, I edged toward him
to see the court's evidence.

It *was* our literature, but it had been photo-
graphically reduced. He could only see a picture
and read the title. The words were too small to

read. I was thankful that at this time I finally had my glasses. This atheistic system was so terrified of the words of a God in whom they didn't believe that they didn't even give the only evidence of our "crime" to the court officials.

"Just what type of flying did you do in Vietnam?" the prosecutor quizzed Mel.

"I was a helicopter test pilot," he responded through the interpreter.

"But we have found that you were an instructor pilot, you trained others to kill, to go into combat," Santos argued triumphantly.

I arose halfway from my bench.

"That's a lie. He was not trained to kill!" I yelled angrily, but was shouted down.

Mel later told me that the Instructor Pilot designation had been entered erroneously in the computer at the Pentagon in Washington. He had tried in vain to have it corrected. How did a Communist court in Havana know that he was listed as an Instructor Pilot on a Pentagon computer? It was a hair-raising thought.

"Just why did you come on this trip? Were you paid?" Santos demanded angrily.

"God sent me on this trip." Mel's voice was calm.

"God?" the prosecutor smiled cynically. Captain Santos then lashed at Mel. "You are a fanatic, too!"

For the next few minutes the prosecutor screamed about aggression in Vietnam and Chile and about the CIA. We left the room after our grilling, wondering if anybody really knew why we were being tried.

Ed Beffel from the U.S. State Department was there taking notes. We didn't know about his presence, nor were we allowed to talk to him. He told Mel later that the event reminded him of the Scopes monkey trial in that it was a legal procedure involving faith and differences in belief.

The prosecutor originally asked for a sentence of from three to twelve years, according to law 1262 of the 1974 Social Defense Code. Current penal law prescribes the making or mere possession of oral or written propaganda "against the socialist order, international solidarity, or the revolutionary state" punishable by three to twelve years deprivation of liberty. In other words, if anything you write or even say differs with the G-2 interpretation, you can and will go to prison.

Another section of the code states: Dissemination of "false news or malicious predictions tending to cause alarm or discontent in the populace" is punishable by one to four years' deprivation of liberty or six to fifteen years if dissemination occurs through the mass media. According to their own law, even if they pervert the intentions of our Christian literature, the maximum we should receive is fifteen years.

We were given twenty-four. In sentencing us, which is done by simply giving notice later at the prison, the tribunal decided to apply law 425 of 1959 dealing with counter-revolutionary activities, with a sentence ranging from twenty years to death. We were thus sentenced to twenty years for "counter-revolutionary activity" plus four years for illegal entry. Although our crossover was legal, our desperate crash on the Cuban coast was not.

We stood in the prison office on the first floor, looking at the sheets of long legal paper. Several pages of charges were filed against us. Two and a half decades of prison? I felt honored. Would God keep me in such a beautiful school for so long? We went back upstairs and told our Christian friends. They hugged us and treated us as royalty.

Later in a conference at the prison with Wayne Smith, head of the U.S. Interests section in Cuba, he mentioned that our cases had bypassed all the courts and gone into the hands of the Council of Ministers. This consists of Fidel Castro, his brother Raul, and two or three yesmen.

"The Council informed me that you are being held in Cuba under extraordinary circumstances," he told us.

This was no surprise. During our time in prison, we met many under the same "circumstances." The extraordinary had become ordinary. Laws in Cuba are only printed as part of the Communist deception and lie. The G-2 apparatus is the law. According to the new Cuban Constitution of 1976, we should have had a trial within twenty days of our arrest. According to Cuban international agreements, prisoners can be subjected to no "degrading treatment" while in prison. In reflecting on this, I could not forget the day I had been placed in a urinal with the hood over my head.

At this point some may protest that the Cuban Constitution guarantees religious freedom. When a deeper study is made, the poison is found in many pockets. In Article 61 of the Constitution, one of the oppressive catch-alls exists: "None of the freedoms which are recognized for citizens may be exercised contrary to what is expressed in the Constitution and the law, or contrary to the existence and objective of the Socialist State, or contrary to the decision of the Cuban people to build socialism and communism."

The Marxists are saying, "You Christians should create an oil which will mix with our water." Some Marxist pastors and some liberal Christians try to do that, exchanging their oil of the Holy Spirit for that of philosophy and dialogue, the oil of discussion.

Article 54 of the Constitution, which mentions religious freedom, is prefaced by this statement: "the Socialist state . . . bases its activity and educates the people in the scientific materialist concept of the universe." Thus my strange discussion with the prosecutor on the subject of life after death. Even this was a political field of battle for him.

We were returned to Combinado to enjoy the prison "verbal library." As in ancient history and among illiterate groups, when there is no printed literature available, human experience, testimony, and memory serve as a rich field of learning. Rudolfo Camps, in prison for ten years, told me of returning to Cuba at night by boat with a racing bicycle on board. Rudý then rode into Havana to get his fiancée. He was apprehended and spent many years in labor camps and prisons.

At a camp called Taco Taco, he was cutting sugar cane when a bull wandered into the circle of prisoners. The animal was quickly hacked to pieces, and the raw flesh carried inside the shirts of the starving men back into the compound. The bones were buried. When planting sugar cane, the prisoner-slaves would eat the roots before pushing the young cane into the ground. Later the authorities would be furious at the great highways of dead yellow cane running through the green fields.

Several jokes have been told in Poland and Romania about bread and meat lines. Cuba has its food joke, too. Fidel Castro sent an agent to Miami to see how the Americans were eating. He stayed in an expensive hotel for a week before returning to Havana.

"You were right, Commander," he joyfully reported. "The situation there is terrible! I entered their best restaurant and ordered mush. There wasn't any. I asked the waitress for old Russian beef. None. 'Well, is there any old pea soup?' Sorry, none available. Getting angry, I asked her in exasperation, 'Well, just what do you have here?' Showing me the menu she pointed to the lobster, steak, and chicken. It was incredible! I told her, 'Wow! Are you people behind the times! We were eating this in Cuba twenty years ago!' "

Most lobster and other such luxury items collected by Soviet-Cuban fishing vessels are processed off-shore and never reach the island, except for the tourist hotels. The best of the grapefruit and most of the mangoes are shipped to Canada.

A quiet old gentleman with snow-white hair was introduced to me as Andres Vargas Gomez. Gomez is the grandson of Maximo Gomez, the Cuban patriot. Andres was reading Thomas a Kempis' book, *The Imitation of Christ.* A writer and attorney, he has been held in prison for more than twenty years. Andres is 65, has only one kidney, has had asthma and other physical problems. But in spite of all this, many times when I was sick he would send me the few eggs he was able to obtain.

During my seventeen months with him, I never saw an angry or bitter expression on his face or heard hatred in his voice. He is a tender, sensitive man who lives and who waits. Andres has a living, personal faith in Christ. He leads the Catholic services held, when possible, in one of the cells. Noble leads the Protestant meetings.

The services are back to back. Most of the thirty or forty men who are able to crowd into the room attend both. The love of Christ and hunger for spiritual food in that starvation environment tend to bring them together in many ways despite strong doctrinal differences.

Many Sunday mornings I was successful in sneaking into their area. In John 8:59 I notice that Jesus had to hide in the midst of persecution. He did so many times as He sought to fulfill His ministry. Jesus is still hiding today. The living Jesus in the hearts of Christians around the world still helps them hide when necessary.

As I was helping Noble prepare the "pulpit"— a bedsheet draped over a board—one of the guards named Pedro rushed into the long room looking for me. He had seen me pass. The men quickly placed me on the top bunk and covered me with a sheet. In this galera of sixty-five men, many were old, sick and paralyzed, and were still in bed. I lay deathly still with my head covered, like one of them.

"All right, where is he? Where is the American?" Pedro fumed. "I know you have him here."

The men said little, joking with him a moment. The roomful of prisoners functioned as a unit, a family, as brothers. Pedro stormed out, unaware that his hand had been resting on my bed as he stared around the room. Once more the Lord Jesus was able to hide, and I was honored that He had protected me in such a miraculous way.

The pastor patiently draped the sheet, pinning it precisely, undoing it, adjusting it in a labor of love. His quiet, patient movements during these moments spoke thousands of sermons to me. He had finally been secretly ordained by ministers

Tierra bendita y divina

Tierra bendita y divina,
es la de Palestina donde nació Jesús.
Benditas son las naciones temblaron
que derraman su luz.

(Coro)

Tú eres la Historia, intervienes,
marcha en tu seno, se derrama
tu sangre preciosa, sangre
del universo, hijo de Dios //

② Cuenta la historia del pasado
que en su seno sagrado
vivió el salvador
y en sus hermosos olivares
habló a las millares
la palabra de Dios.

③ Cuentan todos los ríos
que sus aguas divinas
dan la juventud
Vidas amores desengaños
que si tuvieron vida
mis mañanas también.

Hymnsheets copied on Cuban cigarette paper

FUMAR DAÑA SU SALUD

LIGEROS

LIGEROS

FUMAR DAÑA SU SALUD

20 CIGARRILOS
Extra suaves

coming to "visit" other family members. They had gathered quickly in the big visiting hall, out of sight of the guards, and prayed while laying hands on Noble. This reminded me of David's secret ordination by Samuel in 1 Samuel 16.

The men stood around the walls. Their "hymnals" were miraculously produced, copied on cigarette package paper with a twenty-year-old pen and homemade ink. The beautiful lines and letters were loving works of art—love letters to God. It was Noble's handwriting. He had spent hundreds of hours copying hymns and poems. These, too, would soon be confiscated. But when the words are written on your heart, your treasure is in a secure place.

The singing began, powerful waves of love and victory pouring out of many throats. The amazing sound washed over me. Tears welled in my eyes. I was standing here miraculously in a circle of love and compassion, a little candle in the midst of great, brutal darkness. The impression that spoke most to my heart was power, victory. There was a visible, tangible, power on these men's faces and in their voices. I saw machete scars on their arms. They had heart problems, arthritis; some were crippled. They had few material possessions. In the eyes of most of the world, they had nothing. Yet they had everything.

Noble would speak, wearing a special clean white shirt he had made from a bedsheet. In a quiet, calm voice, always with his brilliant smile, he would speak of Jesus the Prince of Peace,

Jesus the Savior, the King. The men would give requests for prayer, asking help for their families, for their island. Few ever asked for anything for themselves. They bowed their heads, and one would pray . . . for the free world, for America, for Europe, for the Communists.

Delgado and Prado, both with severe heart problems, always stood there together. Little Prado would give me a bear hug every time he saw me. He would smile and say, "Soon we will go together to Miami!" He has been in prison, like many, for twenty years. They both have letters of thanks from President Truman for serving in the American Navy.

Once, the head of our floor, Lieutenant Calzada, was on duty during the church service. He had boasted of being a woman-and-baby-killer in Angola—anything to further the revolution. Surprising us, he strode arrogantly into the cell and demanded that the service be stopped immediately. One of the Christians pulled out a copy of the *Granma*, Cuba's Communist newspaper, and showed him the back page. Many sections of the *Granma* are prepared carefully for export, as was this one.

"Look, you have a picture of a church," the believer declared. "It says here that there is freedom of religion in Cuba. So why do you go against what the Party newspaper says?"

The religious article was in answer to a letter from a Caribbean inquirer who doubted that religious freedom exists.

The *Granma* is such a rich source of fiction

and lies that a special joke has been created for it: Napoleon, the French Emperor, after his sad defeat at Waterloo, had a meeting with modern-day world leaders. He spoke to Brezhnev:

"If I had had your mighty Red Army, I could have defeated the English."

"Da," said the Russian leader, "that is true."

Napoleon then addressed President Carter: "If I had had your cruise missile, the victory at Waterloo would have been mine." Carter agreed.

Then turning to Fidel Castro, Napoleon smiled, "Fidel, if I had had your newspaper the *Granma*, the world never would have known that I lost the battle at Waterloo."

Lieutenant Calzada was backed into a corner momentarily by a lie: the newspaper's lie had trapped him. He retreated, but returned a few weeks later, confiscating all the hymnbooks and other religious materials. Hundreds of hours of handcopying were lost. But God honors our love and effort. I was able to sit with Noble a few hours and help him recopy them, word for word, line by line, verse by verse. The old hymns which I had sung for many years began to take on a new light. Their words and message became more deeply engraved on my heart.

People wonder how many Christians are imprisoned in Cuba. In only one wing of my building, I knew of eleven strong believers from different denominations and about forty others who professed. Twenty-four such wings exist at Combinado del Este. Combinado holds seven thousand or more prisoners. Cuba has between

forty to fifty such institutions, with an esti-
mated population of 300,000 to 450,000, about
five percent of the total populace. Because reli-
gious· prisoners are now mixed with common
criminals, it is impossible to know exactly how
many are there.

Mel and I felt at home among the Cubans. Mel
was handicapped, not knowing Spanish, but began learning from Major Montero Duque. Vargas
Gomez helped me. Mel and I both were able to
speak at the little church services which they
held. We also began having services of our own
in an international wing. When the cells were
unlocked for fifteen minutes, some Africans
from Tanzania and Zaire, Colombians, a Bolivian, a Jamaican, some Americans, and others
visited our little cell for a time of singing, prayer
and study.

Glenn Akam helped copy the hymns and read
Scripture, and Mel often gave some devotional
thoughts. We all shared. The Scriptures we studied and discussed were like injections of penicil-
lin and adrenaline. The Holy Spirit used them to
bring healing and strength. We discussed Christian life and conduct, Joseph's submission to
God as a prisoner, loving one's enemies, and
forgiveness.

We thought that the officials weren't taking
much notice until one day Lieutenant Carlos
passed my cell and, looking in, said, "Well,
Thomas, still fighting with your New Testament,
huh?" But because Christians and officials in the
free world were inquiring about our health and

safety, we were usually left alone. Glenn soon had most of his religious booklets confiscated, but they allowed us to keep our Bibles, smuggled earlier between some newspapers during a lax period. The Cubans and others were not so fortunate.

The Bolivian was called out of the building for a visit from his father, a Communist living in Nicaragua. Lieutenant Carlos, along with his father, told him, "If you continue attending those church meetings you will spend your entire twelve-year sentence here. If you turn and become revolutionary, we'll let you go within a year."

All religion, including the Bolivian's encounter with Christ, represented a political-economic danger. Lenin said, "Communism without atheism is meaningless." The economics of the Communist state depend on massive, co-ordinated obedience. Marxist materialism, an atheistic god, channels the masses in their anthill task of fulfilling the current economic plan without soul-searching interruptions. They have no personal destiny. Only a great mindless collective exists. Lenin knew that co-existence between the Marxist god and God was impossible.

The young Bolivian's brother had fought with Che Guevara, the Argentine rebel. Their family came to Cuba, where he enrolled in the university and learned about the true revolution: special stores only for Communist party members and tourists, and the two-percent elite hierarchy of police and officials who lived many times better than the general population. Seeing the inequalities, he mentioned this in a classroom. Now he was learning that only among prisoners was there equality, and in many ways more freedom. Here he could talk freely. On the street, he couldn't.

He stopped openly attending the services but continued to read the verses and notes. I pray that God will strengthen him in this mighty conflict. As in many other cases, his family had become the enemy. Jesus prophesies in Matthew 10:36, "A man's foes shall be they of his own household."

The same was true of Isidro, a young Cuban boy called the "midget" because of his short stature. He would run up and hug me and begin repeating the Lord's Prayer, which he tried to learn in English.

"Hey, Mr. Religious," he would say to me, "when I get out of here I'm going to your church." Isidro had scars on his back from being beaten by the guards with an automobile fan belt. His father, a Communist, never visited him.

During an exercise period on the large concrete patio (three hours a week), I met another Cuban pastor, Pedro de Armas. Pedro is the president of the Seventh Day Adventists in eastern Cuba. Time came for their annual convention. The State did not want Pedro to be the main speaker because his church had been growing in spite of opposition.

Invoices were stolen from the furniture factory where Pedro worked, and he was accused of embezzlement. Imprisoned for six months during the time of the convention, he was terrified. Officially there are no more political or religious convictions, so Pedro was placed at the mercy of murderers, thieves, syphilitics, and homosexuals in his cell.

From the patio I would speak words of encouragement to him as he cautiously came to the front of his cell. In his sixties, with grey hair and thick glasses, he would peer out with a smile on his face and talk quickly in whispers before the prison trustee came by. The criminals would treat him more brutally at times than the guards. Men were killed almost every night in homosexual love triangles and disputes over possessions.

After six months in prison, Pedro went to court and was found not guilty. Such a wonderful system of justice! Of course, his release coincided with the time that the church convention was over. These "coincidences" happen to people of all denominations, both Catholics and Protestants. When religious or human rights groups investigate these things, they are told by Cuban religious and government officials that there are no Christians in prison. The lie is that all are considered criminals or are placed there for a civil offense. These civil offenses are never deeply investigated.

Here is another type of "civil" offense: Cuban citizens must forego the observance of holy days when they coincide with work or patriotic celebrations. Cuba now has a patriotic celebration lasting exactly one week, celebrating the victory at the Bay of Pigs: *La Semana de Giron.* This observance, by law, takes precedence over the celebration of Easter—the week of the triumphal entry, death, and resurrection of Christ. The coincidence of these dates provides a direct, planned attack to keep Christians from honoring or remembering this period of Christ's life.

What are the "civil" consequences of this spiritual war? Parents who decide to keep their children at home to observe religious holidays may be subject to imprisonment of from three to nine months under two separate provisions, Article 247 (abuse of religious freedom) and Article 365 (acts contrary to the normal development of minors, inducing minors to refuse to fulfill educational work). Article 365 sounds harmless, even beneficial. But it and other laws are mixed, used, and misused to lay traps for believers. Glycerin is harmless, as is nitrogen. Tourists and casual religious observers visiting Communist countries glimpse them in two separate bottles. The Christian who lives in these countries is confronted daily by the mixture—nitroglycerin, an explosive.

I asked many of the men how the Church is able to evangelize and reach the people with so many forms of subtle and overt persecution. Then I learned the beautiful story of the women. The men in Cuba who have a job must be at work or have a medical excuse to avoid going to jail for shirking their "right" to work. Some women therefore have more mobility. They go by twos—modern day disciples—to other provinces to visit a cousin or aunt and talk to them in their homes about the Lord.

In Cuba there are no Christian bookstores, no Christian radio or television stations, no films or developed programs for children, and no Christian touring groups. In Acts 20:20, Paul mentions how he taught from "house to house." Why was this necessary? The Church under the emperors suffered many of the same things that the Church now endures under Communism. But the evil today is greater and more widespread.

Matthew 10:21 says that the children will cause their parents to be put to death. In Cuba the visiting women do not witness to their relatives if a child is present unless they have first talked privately with the parents. The child, usually wearing the red necktie of the Young Pioneers, is trained to report superstitious gatherings to his school teacher or to the CDR family living on each block—the Committee for the Defense of the Revolution.

Children who accept Christ and mention this at school, refusing to wear the red necktie, are many times placed in *pupilo potestades*. These are State-run schools with room and board. Away from their families, they learn the religion of Marx and Lenin instead. I refer not to Communism under Stalin during the "bad old days." I speak of *now*, the 1980s.

The following is a section of a statement

made by the First National Congress on Education and Culture in Havana, April 30, 1971. The
Communists during this period were worried
about the Church's influence over the youth
and, during this convention, implemented "a
child-stealing" policy. This is now proving to be
quite effective. Here are their own words:

> ". . . The church's proselitistic activity
> among children and the church's activism
> through organization of sports and social
> functions underlines the fact that our work
> is insufficient and that the enormous
> potential resources of the Revolution that
> could be used by the political and mass
> organizations and the schools are not uti-
> lized . . . the programming of extra curricu-
> lar activities and attention to children and
> youth and the organization of free time
> and recreation time as a policy to be fol-
> lowed, will be a definite solution for these
> problems. . . ."

So the Church is a problem. State programs of
diversion are in full swing in Cuba. School pic-
nics, sports events, and weekend trips all center
on Sunday. True, in a free society many activities take weak people away from worship. But in
Cuba, these are official school functions, with
the teacher attending, carrying her list of students, and taking roll. It is a socially, scientifi-
cally designed plan to steal and to poison.

If Marxism-Leninism is only a political-economic system, why the continual aggressive anti-God war? It is not a system of logic and law but a hate-filled, fanatical, religious belief. The Cuban Constitution states in Paragraph 3 of Article 54, "It is illegal and punishable by law to oppose one's faith or religious belief in the Revolution."

Wondering about the lack of Bibles and hymnbooks in Cuba, I asked Noble and the others about the problem. I also inquired by various means among Cubans visiting the prison. The information that I gathered was similar to stories I had heard from Romanians, Russians and Bulgarians: "We went to the printer with the money. He said there was time, but we would have to wait until the special paper arrived. We waited. We called back and were told that the paper had come. But the printer sadly mentioned that he now had no time. We waited. When the time was available, the paper had been used by someone else." All print shops are run by the State, by the "people," by the Communist Party, but only for certain people.

Many former church schools are now Communist training centers where atheism is taught. The Baptist seminary in Havana, *Seminario Bautista Loma de Chaple*, is allowed to remain open with its large classrooms, halls and library. It has only seven students—the most permitted by the government.

We joyfully began learning more about the aerial "print shop" I had been using across Cuba.

Another symbol of Castro's stranglehold on Christians. Few students are allowed to attend this once thriving seminary.

Two prisoners from Matanzas, who had been held there for many years, were transferred to our floor. Matanzas was near the route I had taken with John on December 7, 1978. Would they know anything? I walked in the middle of four of my Cuban brothers to meet them. I kept my head down since I was taller than they, and shuffled along. At the end of the hall we met and embraced.

I asked them about the time when we had made the flight. The morning after our drop, I was told, thousands of the leaflets were found by swimmers, tourists, and Cuban workers on Veradero Beach. The police sent several car loads of zealous young internal security men to run up and down the beaches and in the fields to confiscate the material. This only drew more attention to the unusual event. I was once again thrilled to hear that the police were picking up some of the literature. They always read it and sometimes keep a piece of it before turning the rest over to their superiors.

We learned later that we had not just covered the north beach, which was our point of exit, but had left a line widely scattered by the wind across the entire island. The leaflets were found and distributed among Cuban farmers. Once again a beautiful confirmation! This school of His continued to be a rewarding, joyous one, in spite of the physical difficulties.

During this month, I began receiving reports from Camaguey. Eighty percent of the families who visited the prison and who lived in our drop zone either had a piece of the literature in their homes or knew where to find some. Ranchers discovered it in their cow pastures. The roofs and streets of Ciego de Avila had been covered by our "tropical snowfall." Castro called a special meeting in this city and tried to counteract the effects of our trip. Here, too, our missiles of love had exploded. God's message had struck terror to the heart of communism. His Word had brought hope to the souls of the people.

Mel and I rejoiced at the magnitude of our success. Every agonizing moment of our ordeal was worth it.

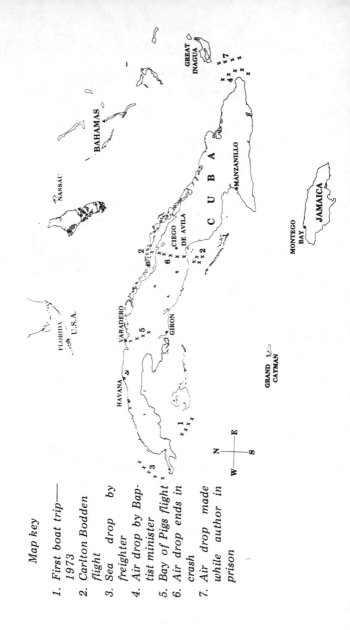

Map key

1. First boat trip—1973
2. Carlton Bodden flight
3. Sea drop by freighter
4. Air drop by Baptist minister
5. Bay of Pigs flight
6. Air drop ends in crash
7. Air drop made while author in prison

10

Guard Towers, Our Church Spires

The physical situation inside the prison usually matched the political climate outside, thus contributing to an unstable set of circumstances. Policy is based on the whims and emotions of Castro rather than on law or precept.

In the fall of 1979, as the world learned more of the Russian troop presence in Cuba, we had our communication lines cut with the U.S. Interest Section. We were allowed the monthly visit, but no letters were passed.

Our cell, number 14, was attacked one night by Cuban prisoners, mainly homosexuals. They first cut the power to the room, then hurled several glass bottles through the bars. They broke through our cell door in the midst of screams, flying glass, and knives made from cafe-

teria trays. I was carried in the darkness by Indio
to a safe corner of the room. Indio, a Cuban
political prisoner, was the Hercules of our cell-
block. He then picked up a table and threw it
into the faces of the attackers.

Mel was standing nearest the door. Although
others were cut, he didn't receive a scratch.
When faced with such unexpected resistance, the
intruders ran into the dark hallway.

During this period the guards showed abso-
lutely no interest in helping us. To the contrary,
they vanished from the halls, either afraid of the
danger or ordered out of the war. For weeks
afterward, a state of cold war existed. Many
prisoners armed themselves with knives or
spears. The Cubans from Cell 16—politicals—
came to our aid. They worked all night making
weapons. The tension was electric. We had to
keep our own cell door locked with coat-hanger
wire, since no guards would protect us.

Later in May of 1980, when Castro cleaned
out the prisons and sent thousands of prisoners
to the United States, none of the political prisoners were allowed to leave. Many of our
attackers were released instead.

Death and disfigurement at the hands of the
guards came just as often as from the prisoners.
One afternoon in May of 1980, Lieutenants
Calzada and Galan, among other officials, strode
out onto the concrete patio of Building Two to
"talk" with eighteen *launcheros*. While Castro
permitted the release of prisoners to the United
States, none of those imprisoned for trying to

escape the island were allowed to go. Others, mostly common criminals, were forced out under threat that they would serve every day of their sentence behind bars if they refused.

By cracking the raw whip of power, the Cuban State continued to pour out its cup of bitterness. The *launcheros*, quite rightly feeling cheated, wished to discuss the matter. Calzada, Galan, and others came to the "discussion" with steel cables, machetes, clubs and belts. They waded into the men, swinging their sporting instruments. Three *launcheros* died, one with brain tissue hanging out of his skull. Several others were carried away with severe multiple cuts.

That same week the American prisoners listened to Cuban radio and television assail President Jimmy Carter, Vice President Walter Mondale and National Security Advisor Zbigniew Brezezinski with filthy names. A political cartoon of Carter in the Communist newspaper *Granma* depicted him on all fours in a homosexual position. Many more cartoons depicted American officials among flies and excrement.

The Americans in Building Two peacefully demonstrated against this mockery by refusing to eat supper. In ten minutes, about sixty guards marched onto the floor wearing gas masks, carrying clubs, mace, bayonets, and accompanied by dogs. All Americans were led to the punishment cells, where for fifteen days they slept in filth on concrete floors. All concluded, from the looks in the guards eyes, a stabbing or beating could have been a reality. During previous years, some had been stabbed, beaten, and kept in cells full of water for days until their skin peeled.

During this time, I was across the street in the hospital with Walter Clark. I was able to enter the hospital through the help of a fellow prisoner, Dr. Jorge Torriente, who was on the hospital staff for a short time. Several medical doctors were in the prison. I had experienced a great weight loss because the food we received was very poor.

The fish that arrived on our floor looked as if it had been part of a prehistoric exhibit. We learned that it came to the kitchen frozen in boxes from the Soviet Union, dated 1971, nine years old. The rice from China contained so many rocks that one ate at great risk. Glenn chipped and broke his teeth many times. The mush and pea soup and rancid Russian beef were all old, tired staples. We rarely saw the beef, although two weeks before our release we received it every day.

My transfer to the hospital was motivated by more than physical problems. I received a note from a prisoner there named Armando Valladarez. Armando is a poet who has been held for twenty years, seven years in a wheelchair. In all that time he had never been allowed to see his wife, Marta. His love for God and man is infectious, and his joy and zest for living are incredible. Although he suffers from asthma, high blood pressure, and paralysis from the waist down, Armando is such a fountain of songs and

jokes and stories and blessings that many of the
hospital staff and many of the guards try to visit
him, though it is forbidden. His photo is under
the glass of the desk of the commander of the
guards, warning everyone that he is a dangerous
counter-revolutionary agent. A *dangerous* poet
in a wheelchair!

Upon meeting Armando in Ward C, I had to
look through two additional sets of bars to a
solitary room where G-2 holds the "vicious"
criminal. His therapy equipment, donated by
concerned organizations in the West, was thrown
into the corner of the room, a pile of useless
junk, after being officially accepted by penal
authorities. His poetry about suffering, love,
God, and the human spirit make him a living
bomb to the Castro government. He doesn't fit
the automated Marxist mold.

I found a kindred spirit in Armando, who
exhibited a love for God, beauty and man, and a
hatred for atheistic poison. He told me of his
time in the great prison on the Isle of Pines.
Tourists are now shown the five huge circular
buildings and told that they were Batista's buildings. More Cubans were held there under Castro's administration than at any other time. The
hunger was incredible. In anger and desperation,
Armando bit the head off a snake he found in
the sugar cane.

The commander of the prison had a pet pig
which wandered between the five towers, root-
ing around for food. One afternoon a noose was
lowered through the barred windows of the

third floor and the pig, squealing in surprise, was rapidly hoisted forty feet in the air. Too large to be hauled through the metal grate, he was quickly butchered while hanging outside the window. The pieces of pork were pulled inside, cooked, and eaten so fast that when the guards arrived fifteen minutes later only the smell remained.

I learned of the death of Reverend Alfredo Ramero, a Cuban pastor and graduate of the West Indies Bible Institute. Ramero had died in his cell from brucellosis after six years of detention at *El Principe* Prison in Havana. Another Bible preacher, Gerardo Gonzales Alvarez, was called "Brother in the Faith" by his fellow prisoners. A godly man, he was martyred on September 1, 1975, during the infamous massacre at Boniato Prison. Armando later smuggled his testimony out of Cuba. Here is the translation as Armando wrote it:

The Brother in the Faith

That Saturday, the groups of prisoners were returning early, at dusk. Thousands of prisoners, surrounded by rifles and bayonets, were silently arriving from the forced labor camps, forming tight lines of hunger, sweat and fatigue. All of them dirty, some were barefoot, and others wore ragged clothes. Their shoulders were fallen, their backs bent as if they were carrying all bitterness and misery.

The muddy streets and roads which led to the penitentiary on the Isle of Pines, and those inside, surrounded by high wire fences, were filled with long columns of men who had just finished the sweltering journey through the mosquito-infested swamps, the quarries, and the citrus plantations fertilized by our blood. More than six thousand political prisoners were housed in this gigantic concentration camp. Some had already entered the building. The prisoners, undernourished, and with the weariness of centuries, were walking slowly. The voices of the section head were heard yelling for them to hurry. That was normal, the same litany every day, month after month, year after year. Then the guards would beat those leading the march with bayonets and clubs, and the line would advance a little faster. Block twenty six, with its four sections, advanced slowly down the road which was parallel to our building. They were exhausted. More than walk, they dragged, without strength to raise their legs.

The guards demanded more speed in their march, threatening them by stirring their machetes and bayonets in the air. The prisoners tried to comply, but the guards demanded more and began beating.

"Hurry, up you s.o.b.'s," they shouted

while unleashing their fury and cowardice. The machetes and bayonets made a slapping sound on the back[s] of the prisoners. There was a commotion in the line, a disturbance. The guards lunged into them and continued beating with fury and violence. The first ones made a superhuman effort, then withdrew from their beatings. Suddenly, while his back was slapped with the machete, a prisoner raised his hands and eyes to Heaven and shouted, "Forgive them Lord, for they don't know what they do."

It was as if the back on which the machete fell once and again, ripping up the skin, was not his. The clear eyes of the "Brother in the Faith" shone, his arms opened toward Heaven imploring forgiveness for his torturers. At that moment he was an unbelievable, supernatural, marvelous man. The cap fell off his head, exposing his grey hair. Very few who met him knew his real name. He was as a limitless fountain of faith which he passed on to his fellow prisoners in their most difficult and desperate situations.

"Have faith, brother . . ." he repeated constantly, leaving on his way a trail of optimism and peace. We all called Gerardo simply, "Brother in the Faith."

A Protestant pastor, he had dedicated his life to preach the Word of God. His most beautiful sermon was himself. When he arrived at the Cabaña fortress, there were thousands of prisoners crowded in the narrow wards. They slept on the floor, in the corners, under the beds. Fear and death visited every night because there were executions three times. We never knew if we would see again the prisonmate who was taken to the Communist tribunals.

The Soviet rifles' discharges broke in pieces the Cuban chests which dared confront the atheistic dictatorship of slavery. Those centennial moats trembled with the viril shouts of "Death to communism, Hail Christ the King!"

In those instants of tremendous agony, the Brother in the Faith raised his arms toward the invisible Heaven beyond the vaults, "Lord, receive him in your arms!" And then, when we could hear the sound of the hammers nailing the coffins, the Brother in the Faith told us that the prisoner was privileged because God had called him to His side. He helped many to confront death with bravery and serenity. And so he went among the groups, reaffirming their faith, quieting their spirits, giving them comfort and support.

Every day, when the galleys were opened, he went around looking for the sick. Whether they wanted or not, he washed their dirty clothes. Anyone could see him there, with a piece of rough cloth or leftover nylon tied to his waist as an

apron, facing mountains of clothes . . . tall
and bent over the washbasin, sweating in
profusion. His hair was white and in his
clear eyes a resplendent light shown.

He used to get us out of our bunks to
attend the worship services.

"Get up, lion's cub, the Lord is calling
you," he would call.

To the Brother in the Faith we could not
say no. If he found someone in a thought-
ful or saddened mood, he would tell him:
"I want to see you in the service this afternoon . . ." and that one had to go.

His sermons had a primitive charm, he
had an extraordinary magnetism. From a
pulpit improvised with a few old boxes
covered with a sheet and a simple cross, the
thundering voice of the Brother in the
Faith delivered his daily preaching. Then
we all sang hymns of praise to God, which
he inscribed on cigarette covers and distributed among the attendants. Many times
the guards dispersed those prayer minutes
with beatings and blows from their rifle
butts, but they couldn't frighten him.

When he was taken to the slave work
camps in Isle of Pines, he organized Bible
reading and choral groups. Having a Bible
was a subversive act. He had, we don't
know how, a small one which was always
with him.

If any tired or sick prisonmate was
lagging behind in his furrow or in the

amount of stones which he had to break with a sledge hammer, the Brother in the Faith appeared by his side. Thin, strong, he had an amazing endurance for any physical effort, and hastened the other's work, saving him from a beating. When any of the guards went by behind him, and struck him with a bayonet, the Brother in the Faith straightened up like a spring, looked the guard in the eyes and spoke kindly, "May the Lord forgive you . . . !" About a thousand prisoners were in the building. We all felt love and admiration toward this man who didn't deny having been a great sinner.

The work gangs started coming out at five in the morning. We had to gather at the huge central patio under roof and bars. Sometimes a few on the higher levels lagged behind and, when this happened, the garrison guards entered and started beating everyone. There encouraging us was the Brother in the Faith.

"Don't give foot to the devil, brothers. . . ." he told the slow ones.

While we formed the long line for "breakfast"—hot sugared water, which they brought in tanks of fifty-five gallons with the taste of petroleum—the Brother in the Faith often quoted Bible stories, or made us laugh with his original and very personal interpretations about sin and men's behavior.

"Don't forget that I lived in sin, and

knew temptation," he reminded us. His greatest goal was that we would not hate each other. Almost all of his sermons carried this message.

Now he is at the Boniato prison, "Biological Experimentation & Extermination Center," in an enclosed cell, with metal plates. But his voice, as if emerging from the depth of a cave, is heard every afternoon calling for worship and prayer, which he didn't neglect even for a day.

Everyone is quiet. A respectful silence fills the deserted hallways of those catacombs. Estebita, el Pire, and Castillito are already dead. . . . The messages those days brought tears even to the driest eyes. No preacher ever worked for God and men under more adverse conditions. Hunger and sicknesses have undermined his body. He is almost a skeleton, his hair is whiter, and his eyes brighter than ever before.

The garrison is clearing for action, shooting haphazardly. They have already shot some prisoners who are not confined in the front section, and they threw grenades. Inside the cells, closed tightly, one cannot see anything, only hear. And then they begin to open the cells and they bring the prisoners out with blows, shoving them to the end of the hall. They are almost all out; many can barely remain standing and lean against the walls. They are thin, exhausted from the hunger and tortures. The brutal beatings began, mangling arms and ribs, heads and faces; the handicapped are torn from their wheelchairs, pulled by their legs, and kicked on the floor . . . all of a sudden, a prisoner, bone thin, ghostly, with raised arms, interposes himself among the guards who are beating them and yells at an invisible Heaven: "Forgive them Lord, for they know not what they do!" His eyes glow like two flaming fires, and his hair is white. The guards stop a moment at the unexpected scene.

"Forgive them Lord, for they know not what they are doing . . . !"

"Get back!" yells the Communist lieutenant, Raul Perez de la Rosa. The guards draw back and the official pulls the trigger of his Soviet AKM rifle. The first blast climbs up the chest of the Brother in the Faith, searching for his radiant eyes; the second, ripping his neck, almost severs his head from his body.

You forgive them, Brother in the Faith, if you want to, but they do know what they are doing.[1]

How can one physically crush a spiritual power? The Communists are perplexed and furious that, despite their campaigns of diversion, despite oppression, despite substitution of young Marxist pastors in place of Bible-believing

---

[1] From "El Corazon Con Que Vivo" *Ediciones Universal.* P.O. Box 450353, Miami, FL 33145.

Boniato Prison in eastern Cuba, where the Brother in the Faith was martyred.

men, the Church is still thriving. In the Soviet Union the Church is growing many times faster than in Western Europe. As atheistic minds are spiritually darkened, they cannot grasp the concept that the Church is made of "living stones." The Apostle Peter says that we are lively stones built into a spiritual house. I met many of these "stones."

We stand on the Chief Cornerstone: Christ. I had tried to explain this concept many times to Captain Santos, but spiritual food is tasteless, odorless, and colorless to a material man. Perhaps someday his taste buds will awaken, and he will hunger for God.

One day, with a Russian camera smuggled in on a medicine tray, I was able to take Armando's picture, and he took mine. The guards burst into our ward the next day with Lieutenant Castillo, Chief of Security, and found two rolls of blank film in Armando's room. Fortunately they didn't know that a third roll existed, for I had hidden it in my large intestine, tied in the finger of a surgical glove. There I would keep letters to my wife and family, photos, film, and other documents. Once I sent a letter, signed by twelve Christians, detailing the brutal persecution in Cuba.

I also sent out poems. I had written poetry years earlier, and now, as I associated with a poet, God began reviving this within me. One poem was called *Crown of Thorns:*

> *Barbed wire—a crown of*
> > *thorns*
> *Encircles us*
> > *piercing the flesh.*
>
> *Guard towers—our church*
> > *spires*
> *Cause the wounds*
> > *to bleed afresh.*
>
> *We drink His cup*
>
> *His joy we feel*
> > *above the dogs*
> *the screams*

Photos taken with a contraband Russian camera: above, Tom White in prison hospital.

Armando Valladarez, still in his wheelchair, must wait ten more years for freedom.

the clang of steel
As from these tombs
alive we view
the dead outside—
the blind.

Our prayers melt bars
crush concrete too
When weak we find
Our strength in You,
O God.

I attached the camera to a thread and hung it down the airshaft of the guard's bathroom. It was found two days later.

The treatment in the hospital was minimal. In our ward I saw six different illnesses, all being treated with only a bottle of glucose. In my two months there I saw a doctor for five minutes. The test done for my supposed stomach cancer was performed incorrectly.

Walter Clark, the other American in the hospital, was in constant pain because of problems with a back he had broken previously. Not only did the authorities refuse to give him better treatment, but his wife was denied permission to bring his back brace for several months. Walter lay awake many nights in agony, unable to move. As relations between the U.S. and Cuba worsened, his treatment grew more inhumane. For months he still languished there. No doctor saw him. He had to find secret ways to obtain pain pills. He lost more than fifty pounds.

We called the chief surgeon of the hospital "Dr. Club." We had seen him break a large pole over the head of a prisoner nurse named Casavilla. During the medical treatment of some Cuban political prisoners downstairs in the hallway, a disagreement arose between two prisoners. The guards, with their usual overkill tactics, began beating everyone in that section of the hallway. Loyal to Castro, "Dr. Club" began slamming a pole on the heads of patients who were standing on the edge of the fracas.

Another guard called the "Gorilla" knocked off the glasses of Napoles, the volunteer male nurse, cutting him in the face. Mario Chanes was beaten badly. Mario, in prison now for twenty years, was one of the original revolutionaries who came with Fidel Castro on the boat *Granma* to defeat Batista.

The majority of these eighty-three victorious "liberators" are in prison, dead, or living in Miami. Every few years all previous political photos of Fidel with his men have to be doctored, cropped, and redone as more of the faithful become disenchanted with his revolution of the "people." Such is communism, a subtle lie, boiling beneath the surface, then quickly pouring over the rim of supporting political structures, sweeping down like hot lava to consume even its own naive revolutionaries.

Few casual observers ever realize the extent of total control exercised over these people. An information vacuum and the barriers it erects constitute only one example. While in the hospital, I was able to obtain a Cuban high school physical science textbook, which had a chapter on the solar system. The four pages of discussion and the pictures of the moon nowhere mentioned that man had ever been on its surface or that samples of the moon had been brought to Earth. The book contained no lunar photos taken by the Americans.

"Perhaps it's sadly outdated," I muttered, flipping to the front. The date was 1976. The text mentioned that the latest advances made in the acquisition of lunar knowledge are those of the Soviet Union with its satellite Lunik II. Cuba was one of the only two nations of the world which did not televise the lunar landings. This information starvation for ideological reasons runs through the entire spectrum, covering everything from science to religion.

This imposing curtain falls over even the Earth's atmosphere.

Shortwave radios were hidden among us. Guards found one, hidden inside a hollow book, during an intensive search. The authorities knew that we had another, since certain groups of Cubans and Americans were always much better informed about world events than the prison officials or the spies among the prisoners.

I was with Juan Dominguez on several occasions, listening to Christian broadcasts from Bonaire and Quito. Many times they were jammed. Other nights we could find a clear frequency. What a thrill to hear the beautiful, concise messages of hope and love. The singing was sheer joy emanating from that little box to us. We used intravenous tubes with rubber stoppers for earphones. Because the batteries kept weakening, we smuggled in a tiny transformer.

Mel and I once heard on the Voice of America that our wives would be coming to Cuba. Another broadcast mentioned our accident and imprisonment. The frequencies would be jammed by the Soviet equipment placed on Cuba. But with persistence, we could find and be enriched by these illegal broadcasts.

The Cuban Christians and politicals used hand signals at various locations to warn the transcribers, those who wrote down the radio news. The system usually worked smoothly. One afternoon I stood in front of Dominguez to shield him while he listened to a WKWF broadcast from Key West. The news commentator, Susan Grey, was our greatest source of information, since this station is close to Cuba with an *A.M.* frequency. Juan, huddled in the corner and sitting on the floor, listened intently. Suddenly, I heard footsteps behind me. Turning my head slightly and cautiously, I saw a guard approaching, no more than five yards away! We had no warning. I tapped my shoulder with two fingers—our signal. Juan shoved the radio into his shirt, stood up, and began walking away from the guard. I immediately began talking with the man, blocking his view.

"So, when do we get to go outside this week?" I begged cheerfully. "It sure has been awhile."

He only shrugged.

Turning back to follow my friend, I noticed that the earphone cord was dangling behind him like a tail. But we escaped detection. Safe again!

The authorities finally evacuated the entire wing of the fourth floor of Building One in an attempt to find the little box that represented great danger to them. All the men were moved to Building Two and were throughly searched in the process. No one carried the box. It was left hidden somewhere in Building One.

The defenders of the Communist faith spent several months using sledgehammers to break the walls, looking for this little box of plastic and wires which fired spiritual and ideological missiles on their pure society. The dust clouds rose, the hammers continued to pound. Workers dumped piles of mortar and sand in front of the building, to be used in the extensive repairs. Guards used metal detectors to sweep the halls and walls. It was a witch hunt in reverse. The witches were doing the hunting. We don't think they found the radio.

I carried a cylinder containing letters for several months. I sewed it into the crotch of my underwear and wore it constantly. If I were to be temporarily off the floor, I would leave the underwear with Rafael, who would wear it while I was gone.

One afternoon we had a *riqueza*, a search. Usually through the prison grapevine we would know in advance. This time it took us by surprise. All of our doors opened rapidly and officials poured into every room on our wing. Writing at the time, I leaped off the bunk bed and dashed to the filthy hole in the floor in back of the cell, our bathroom, to wash down the letters. Fine. They were gone. The Lieutenant was furious, but what could he do? Beating me would not help. As we all were herded into a common room while the guards checked our cells, I met Rafael. He had been holding my underwear that day.

"Do you have the underwear?" I whispered.

"No, I didn't have time to put it on. They came too fast!" he breathed frantically.

My stomach tightened. Inside the rubber finger sewn into the underwear was a letter concerning new ways to introduce Christian literature into Cuba. If it were found, I would never leave this place. New flights were begun during this time. John Lessing had made a return trip, his wife helping with the gospel literature.

I sat on some rusty bedsprings with Glen and prayed. I talked to Mel, and he prayed. We prayed with our eyes open, so the spies among the prisoners wouldn't know what was wrong.

"Oh, Lord, I believe that You brought me to Cuba," I spoke quietly. "If You want me to stay here and permanently close the door, then I rest in Your will, even if they find it."

I looked outside. The guards were throwing most of our possessions into the hallway, spending much time in each room, even ripping open mattresses.

"Where did you leave the underwear? Is it hidden?" I pressed Rafael.

"No, it's laying at the foot of my bed in plain sight," he sighed, panic-stricken.

I thought of the photos and letters. If the clothing were even touched or picked up, the heavy cylinder would swing suspiciously in the crotch.

"Oh God, even if they pick it up, don't let them see it. Make them blind, Lord, even if they touch it."

After two long hours, we returned to our cells. The underwear was not there. Rafael was getting shaky. But then he found it. It had been moved and thrown to the other side of the cell. The information was intact. God, as always, was in control.

Now I anxiously waited for a family visit. Such visits for prisoners anywhere are looked upon as a moment with another world, a breath of fresh air. They had special significance for us. The news from the other planet—the free society—would be received, shared, passed around, analyzed, picked over, whether it were uplifting or depressing. Many prisoners plunged from the heights of optimistic theorizing to the depths of pessimistic fatalism. Some even became mental vegetables, bedridden and incommunicative.

I grew more grateful each day as I found that marvelous gift of faith within me, the presence of Jesus, was able to sustain me most of the time on a smooth, even plane. I received a total of five visits from my family. The average expense each time was seven hundred dollars, quite expensive for a three-hour session. The families were not allowed to fly independently to Cuba to see us, but had to come as part of an organized tour.

Ofelia, my older brother, my mother, and father all provided a time of love for me through much sacrifice. I was able to send with them hundreds of letters, photos, and the roll of film from the photos taken in the hospital. They became smugglers. I would call them "light-bearers." The letters they carried were not only from me but from American and Cuban prisoners. Countless tears, sighs, laughter, jokes, and kisses passed through those letters from many old grandfathers who have never seen their grandchildren.

When my brother flew to see me, I had the roll of film. Unlike past "mail carrying," this was no ordinary packet of letters, but something which could cause serious problems for either of us. If discovered, these photos of two skinny men in prison hospital pajamas would be regarded as crimes against the State.

My visit day came. The call sounded. I strode with other Americans to Lieutenant Calzada's office to be stripped and searched. I could see many from the Cuban wing, who were not allowed visits, waving goodbye to me. The guard who searched me was the "the Owl," so nicknamed for his baggy eyes. He was drunk much of the time, probably because he didn't enjoy his job. He was the most belligerant and least co-operative among the guards, who also made jokes about him.

On this day I had many letters as well as the film. One of the packets inserted into my colon was so long that it hurt me to sit down.

"Strip!" the Owl ordered gruffly when it came my turn.

Being one of the few Americans to speak Spanish, I tried to distract him with conversation. It was difficult to talk. I also had a piece of razor blade wrapped in yellow paper under my tongue to cut the rubber fingers off of the packets.

"So, how's it going, Abel?" I grinned. He didn't say much, answering only in grunts. "Sure is tough, working on Saturday, huh? When do you get a day off?" (How I wished he had a day off!) Speaking to him in Spanish seemed to soften him up a little. I was praying at the same time.

Even though I was stripped, Abel did not see the tiny black button I had tucked into my anus. The rubber fingers inside my body were tied to this button by string. After this session and before meeting my older brother, I was able to hide, grasp the button, and fish the material out of my colon. Cutting the rubber off, I took the packets and hid them.

After that, the transfer was relatively simple. As usual, he was calm and collected. On a later visit with Ofelia, I gave her four of these fingers.

During our brief moments together, she showed me a tiny plastic packet of purple powder

Author smuggled this letter to his wife by inserting it into his colon in one of these rubber fingers.

closed with a rubber band.

"What's this honey?" I asked, hardly able to contain my curiosity.

"It's powdered grape juice," she smiled. "I thought we could have a communion service together."

I withdrew some choruses and Bible verses in Spanish, written on the small yellow paper, which I had wrapped around the piece of razor blade hidden under my tongue. We sang together quietly a few minutes, "There's Life in Jesus." Then we read Matthew 10:37-39, the same passage that compelled me to fulfill this mission, when otherwise I would have yielded to the comforts of home:

He that loveth father or mother . . . son or daughter more than me is not worthy of me . . . he that taketh not his cross, and followeth after me, is not worthy of me . . . he that loseth his life for my sake shall find it.

These portions had special meaning to both of us. While I agonized in prison, Ofelia also had taken up her cross. She, too, had given her life for the Lord's sake. Though still separated by thousands of miles and my imprisonment, we indeed were finding life as we had never known it before.

As we knelt in the little visit room alone, drinking the juice and eating a small piece of cracker, a sweet peace filled our hearts.

"Lord Jesus," Ofelia cried softly, "we know that You are working Your perfect will here. When it is time to bring Tom home, Lord, we know that You can free him."

"Oh God," I joined, "thank You for this time, this precious time, with Ofelia. Thank You for Your care and protection over her and the children. Keep them constantly in Your hands, sweet Jesus. You are doing such a wonderful job. When this school is over, send me back to them, Lord. Thank You, Jesus."

We parted with no tears, just smiles, thankful for His joy and care.

11

Wind Around the World

I 'll always be thankful to the Lord for send-ing that great crosswind on our last flight, for it carried the gospel message directly over Ciego de Avila. Known only in part to Mel and me, another wind was now blowing around the world, moving hearts to pray for us and to cry out for us. It was the wind of the Holy Spirit.

Many concerned people today have the mis-taken impression that publicity concerning a prisoner in a Communist country will cause the authorities to treat them more harshly. On the contrary, this is usually not the case. Our release is testimony to this. Vasile Rascol was released early from prison in Romania and Georgi Vins was set free and exiled from the Soviet Union because of the pressures of public opinion.

In Australia, after Merv Knight interceded for us, five thousand Australians wrote to their Prime Minister. Christian missions in Holland, Germany, Switzerland, England, Canada, South Africa, and India urged believers to love by moving their lips in prayer, by moving their pens in writing letters, or by making telephone calls. Christians around the world offered the $175,000 that Castro had asked as ransom for us. After Fidel was notified of the deposit in an intermediary bank, he immediately demanded $300,000. This slave trade is carried on daily by the West German government, which spends millions of dollars yearly buying back German descendants who live in the Soviet Union and East Germany.

My parents and others prayed and wept and pounded on Congressional doors. John McLario of Christian Legal Defense was nearly arrested in Havana, simply for mentioning our case. Four weeks before our intended release was announced, the Miami *Herald* published my prison mug shot and the entire five page communique which Mel and I had written the previous year. The letter was published in several Christian and secular Journals. It was even placed in the *Congressional Record* on August 17, 1980, seven weeks before our release was announced.

During the Carter-Reagan presidential race, visible pressure haunted Castro, who hated Reagan. He screamed and raved several times on Cuban television, calling Reagan "Adolf Hitler." Most of us believe that this was a great factor in

our release. The Egyptian Pharoah let the Israel-
ites go for political motives, but God was the
mover.

The backbone of the effort, the real power,
came through millions of Christians moving their
lips in the most potent form of warfare—prayer.
We learned later of tears pouring down the faces
of Africans, Filipinos, Cuban-Americans, elderly
ladies in California, men and women in Texas
and Oklahoma, and teenagers in Florida, all
swinging the sharpest sword ever known to men,
the Sword of the Spirit.

Our official release was announced on October 13 but, because of red tape and lack of
coordination between governments, we languished in prison for two more weeks. This was
an excellent exercise in patience. To be so close,
yet so far—and still twenty-two and a half years
to serve. Of all the Americans imprisoned there,
our case was by far the most serious.

I kept remembering Castro's words concerning our "extraordinary circumstances." Yet I
knew that God was able. This also was a time of
tremendous tensions, emotional highs, and
gloomy lows for many. All our towels, little
rags, and personal effects left behind during our
three "releases" had been confiscated. Much anger, fear, hope, and joy coursed unchecked up
and down the halls.

Matt and other Americans excitedly showed
me a two-month old message from a Florida
church. The prayer group had promised to pray
for us "until October 15." Prison Colonel

Pacheco Silva officially notified us on that date.
God, not Pacheco, was in control.

I did my usual daily exercises with Glenn,
exchanged notes and comments with Mel about
the latest news, and tried to live normally. But
hope continued to gush up like a second heart
tearing its way through my chest. All of us tried
not to build hope castles. We didn't want to be
hurt later, if a crash were coming. Indeed, on
one of our false releases, as we went back into
the prison, many expressed anguish and pain. I
continually "worked" at resting in the Lord.
The best way was, once again, through song.

The hymn sung at my baptism was "Where He
Leads Me I Will Follow." I sang it as I walked.
When hot and cold emotions would flash at me
from other prisoners or from within my own
soul, I would remember the song. I chewed it,
swallowed it, believed it.

Mel and I could be jerked out of line at any
time. The Communists delight in psychological
warfare. Christians ready to graduate from their
universities have been told the day before, "No
diploma for you." Cuban prisoners whose names
I knew were on release lists have packed their
things only to be told on the day of freedom,
"Sorry, your name isn't here." All had been
devilishly planned beforehand.

Yet we continued to prepare for our release
because we believed it could come any time. Mel
smuggled his Bible over to the Cuban prisoners.
Although their Christian literature is confiscated, especially any English material, we pray

that the Bible remains safe. My Bible also went to another prisoner. I prepared packets of letters from my Cuban brothers and, when the final call came, inserted them into my body.

Our prison buses went directly to Havana airport, where we were taken to the Air Florida chartered jet waiting to take us home. A few carloads of G-2 and other officials parked near us. We said little, for even now, as we started to file onto the plane, they could jerk us out of line. "Sorry, there's been some mistake. White! Bailey!" But no, no such words. We stepped on board and fastened our seat belts, amazed at the clean carpets, air-conditioning and gentle, courteous airline attendants! They smiled. They cared. But we were still in Cuba.

The whine of the engines starting up sent thrilling chills through me. With a roar, the Boeing 737 taxied impatiently to the end of the runway, turned, then rolled, faster, faster, faster, tropical plants and palm trees flashing by!

"Go baby, go! Move . . . move . . . punch it . . . punch it . . . push that throttle!" It seemed that our shouts and tears urged the plane off the runway even quicker. I peered down on the island thinking of Noble, Vargas, Armando, and the others, the new part of my family that I was leaving behind.

Landing in Tamiami, a small airport south of Miami, we taxied up to hundreds of anxious reporters and whirring cameras. A large banner was being held by two women—Ofelia and Mary, our wives.

Mel and Mary Bailey
Sheila and David

"Welcome home, Mel and Tom, there is no God like ours!" it read. A little boy in red overalls played with his big sister on the grass in front of the sign.

"Hey, you guys!" I laughed and yelled to the others in the cabin, "You see that boy? Look at him! Yeah, the one over there. He's mine! His name is Daniel. And that's Dorothy and my wife, Ofelia. . . ."

Each prayer, each article, each letter written

about us while in prison, each word spoken now, reminds me of a carpenter with strong, rough hands holding a shiny nail precisely over a penciled X mark. Swiftly, smoothly and decisively he drives the nail into the board. Another nail, and another, hammered with patience, determination and skill. Our great Carpenter wants us to act thus, with wisdom learned from our instruction manual, the Bible, with a smoothness obtained by the Holy Spirit's gentle influence. Each day we take the nails He gives us and we hit the mark.

Since leaving Cuba, I have been tempted at tiring times to lay the hammer aside, and put the nails in a drawer. Life outside the prison is much more complex. Many issues, all equally important, confront the Christian worker and family every day.

But as I look back and see the gracious and merciful hand of God on my life in this specialized area, I see that He had given me a hammer, one which fits my grip and which is the right weight for me to carry. My personal X mark is over Cuba and other Communist countries, where thousands of my brothers and sisters suffer in prison. The extremely short span of my life on Earth will not change the great course of any nation. But God does not ask that of me. He asks for my heart. Only that.

A few months before that last flight over Cuba, I attended a dinner where the speaker gave an illustration which has a rich meaning for me. It became a prophecy of sorts, and it still applies.

"A little bird became alarmed by a great forest fire," he began. "The bird flew to a nearby stream and returned to the fire each time, releasing a small drop of water from her beak. The tremendous fire paid no attention. On the contrary, the bird's wings became badly singed. But she kept returning even though no visible progress was made against the flames. Finally, caught in a net, the bird died. But she did not lose the battle. God had not asked for progress. He asked for a loving heart. The bird won."

Compassion for those in trouble is at the heart of the gospel. Christian love implies sacrifice. "Remember them that are in bonds, as bound with them; and them which suffer adversity, as being yourselves also in the body," Paul wrote. "To do good and to communicate forget not: for with such sacrifices God is well pleased" (Hebrews 13:3, 16).

During World War II, Christians who showed their protest of the Nazi persecution of the Jews wore the Star of David. They were ready to lay down their lives for these downtrodden people. Our Christian brethren suffering persecution and torture at the hands of the Communists know the meaning of sacrifice well.

I have seen the marks that the oppressors have put on God's people. Many of the persecutions we read of in the Bible take place today behind the Sugar Cane Curtain and in Communist lands around the world. The dire suffering laid upon otherwise ordinary persons produces examples of faith never to be forgotten. It was with great meaning that the Apostle Paul said, "I bear in my body the marks of the Lord Jesus Christ."

We can be a friend of the martyrs in many ways. First, by prayer. God is doing a tremendous work among the believers in Cuba, but He has put into our hands the task of holding these dear ones up with our prayers. We can intercede for Christian leaders, churches and prisoners. We can pray for the Communists, and for the more than ten million Cubans under their boots.

Second, by thinking creatively. With our marvelous brains, we can imagine, create, build, work, and potentially accomplish mighty acts. I am dedicated to making the burdens of the Cuban Church lighter. We have the Spirit, the love, the technology, the energy, the time. God has the resources, the power, the wisdom. Together we can carry the warmth and hope of His Word to our brethren in bonds.

Third, by writing letters. Cuban Communist authorities are afraid of and amazed by our light. They recognize the awesome power of these missiles of yet another kind. Our letters bring hope and courage to believers starved for the fellowship of loving, caring Christians in free lands.

Fourth, by investigating the plight of the martyrs. Conflicting reports and opinions on the true condition of the persecuted Church can leave us confused and uncertain of our task. Uncovering the truth will make us more effective in our outreach.

Fifth, by supporting Christian groups who legitimately buy air time for Spanish gospel radio broadcasts into Cuba. In cancer treatment, the tumor is bombarded with powerful radiation. These broadcasts and other efforts at penetrating the Sugar Cane Curtain with the gospel are mighty bombardments against the Communist cancer in Cuba. No place on Earth can escape the powerful radio waves of Jesus. Thanks to that unstoppable preacher—the radio—God's Word can be heard in the remotest villages.

God can use each of us, whether in our arm chairs or in our airplanes, to fulfill His great commission as a spiritual invasion force! The time is short. We are in a race. The baton is in our hands. The finish line is before us.

While attending a recent National Religious Broadcasters Conference in Washington, D.C., I dreamed that I was standing on a red clay dirt road, looking down at my feet. For some reason I was wearing track shoes, although I don't know how they got on my feet. They were untied. I bent down to tie them, swiftly tugging at the white laces, enjoying the snug fit. Straightening up, I saw my brother Noble with his smiling black face, balding Cleto, skinny old Martell, and white headed Vargas sprinting up behind my right shoulder. They paused a moment beside me, wearing hand-made prison uniforms, white shirts and shorts from bed sheets. They said nothing, just gazed at me expectantly. We began running down the road . . . together . . . in the race.

I wondered what my dream meant.

A television station from the U.S. soon will beam Christian good news and hope toward Havana. The race?

Approximately 80,000 tourists visit Cuba each year. How many would carry a single, tiny Gospel of John in their coat pocket? The race?

Who will sacrifice? Running can be painful, but oh, so exhilarating!

Cuba is an island surrounded by chains of water. The favorite chorus we sang in prison, which always is a spiritual reality and sometimes a physical one, was *"Cristo Rompe Las Cadenas!" Christ Breaks the Chains!* I can see the race now, in that television station, in those tourists, in our letters, in our prayers, in the many other ways that God will reveal whereby we may bring liberty to that island of bondage.

We won't merely break a nice ribbon at the end of this contest. But our chests, full of the Holy Spirit, will break many chains.

Epílogue

I wrote this poem in Building Two on the fourth floor of Combinado del Este Prison.

I dedicate it to my brothers and sisters in Christ on the prison island of Cuba, those who victoriously greet us today through 2 Corinthians 6:5, 10: "In stripes, in imprisonments, in tumults, in labors, in watchings, in fastings . . . as sorrowful, yet always rejoicing, as poor, yet making many rich; as having nothing; and yet possessing all things."

Bars of Light

Bars of light
Cut through our steel cathedral

Sun ray fingers
Slice across the hall
And linger
On faces sanctified.

Free
From anger, fear and hate
Washed clean inside
We sing
And wait.

We sigh
But grin
Knowing that God
Will fill
Our lungs again.

THE SPIRITUAL BATTLE FOR CUBA

Living Testimonies of Faith Under Fire From The Cuban Church Entering The 1990's

For more than thirty years, Fidel Castro tried to extinguish the light of the church in Cuba.

Its glow flickered, but did not go out.

Political and spiritual leaders in this Communist stronghold want the West to believe that religious persecution does not exist. In this book you will learn the truth.

- Discover the true plight of the Cuban church
- See why persecuted Christians around the world regard Cuban believers as comrades in suffering
- Admire the bravery of Cuban pastors
- Witness the outpouring of God's Spirit on Cuba's spiritually famished people

The events presented in this book were taken from the wire services, news articles from three continents, written and verbal reports of pastors and professors who visited Cuba, personal interviews, and taped and written testimony from Christians living behind the Sugar Cane Curtain.

This book does not seek to dramatize the events. All conversations and actions of Cuban authorities and the church occurred as written. The names of the police and Christians are real.

Many pastors in Cuba are not cowards. After more than three decades of control, increasing numbers of Cuban Christians have no fear of reprisal.

This is their story.

In the USA order from:
The Voice of the Martyrs
PO Box 443
Bartlesville, OK 74005